BEING

REFLECTED

UPON

ALSO BY ALICE NOTLEY

165 Meeting House Lane • 1971

Phoebe Light • 1973

Incidentals in the Day World • 1973

For Frank O'Hara's Birthday • 1976

Alice Ordered Me to Be Made • 1976

A Diamond Necklace • 1977

Songs for the Unborn Second Baby • 1979

Dr. Williams' Heiresses • 1980

When I Was Alive • 1980

How Spring Comes • 1981

Waltzing Matilda • 1981, reissued 2003

Tell Me Again • 1982

Sorrento • 1984

Margaret & Dusty • 1985

Parts of a Wedding • 1986

At Night the States • 1988

From a Work in Progress • 1988

Homer's Art • 1990

The Scarlet Cabinet (with Douglas Oliver) • 1992

To Say You • 1993

Selected Poems of Alice Notley • 1993

Close to me & Closer . . . (The Language of Heaven) and *Désamère* • 1995

The Descent of Alette • 1996

etruscan reader vii (with Wendy Mulford and Brian Coffey) • 1997

Mysteries of Small Houses • 1998

Byzantine Parables • 1998

Disobedience • 2001

Iphigenia • 2002

From the Beginning • 2004

Coming After: Essays on Poetry • 2005

City Of • 2005

Alma, or The Dead Women • 2006

Grave of Light: New and Selected Poems, 1970–2005 • 2006

In the Pines • 2007

Above the Leaders • 2008

Reason and Other Women • 2010

Culture of One • 2011

Songs and Stories of the Ghouls • 2011

Secret I D • 2013

Negativity's Kiss • 2014

Manhattan Luck • 2014

Benediction • 2015

Certain Magical Acts • 2016

Eurynome's Sandals • 2019

For the Ride • 2020

The Speak Angel Series • 2023

Early Works • 2023

Runes and Chords • 2023

Telling the Truth as It Comes Up • 2023

BEING
REFLECTED
UPON *(a memoir of 17 years, 2000–2017)*

ALICE NOTLEY

PENGUIN POETS

PENGUIN BOOKS
An imprint of Penguin Random House LLC
penguinrandomhouse.com

LIBRARY OF CONGRESS CATALOGING-IN-PUBLICATION DATA
Names: Notley, Alice, 1945– author.
Title: Being reflected upon: (a memoir of 17 years, 2000–2017) /
    Alice Notley.
Description: New York: Penguin Poets, 2024.
Identifiers: LCCN 2023035950 (print) | LCCN 2023035951 (ebook) |
    ISBN 9780143137979 (trade paperback) |
    ISBN 9780593512067 (ebook)
Subjects: LCSH: Notley, Alice, 1945– | Poets, American—20th
    century—Biography. | LCGFT: Autobiographies. |
    Autobiographical poetry.
Classification: LCC PS3564.O79 B45 2024 (print) |
    LCC PS3564.O79 (ebook) | DDC 811/.54 [B]—dc23/eng/20231018
LC record available at https://lccn.loc.gov/2023035950
LC ebook record available at https://lccn.loc.gov/2023035951

Printed in the United States of America
1st Printing

Set in Dante MT Pro with Ministry Light
Designed by Sabrina Bowers

Acknowledgments

Some of these poems have appeared in the following publications: *A) GLIMPSE) OF)*, *Aphros*, *Arts & Letters*, *Australian Book Review*, *Brooklyn Rail*, *datableed*, *Dusie*, *Gramma Poetry*, *Interim*, *Kenyon Review*, *Paris Review*, *Poem-a-Day*, *Poetry London*, *Spacecraft*, *Splinter*, *Three Fold*, and *Wretched Strangers*.

To Anne Waldman

Contents

Preface   xiii

That Kind of Poem   1

Winter 2013   2

Gravel Ghost or Gravel Gertie   3

Agamemnon   4

Don't Look At   6

Remaking our substance and form   7

Archival Quality I Remember   8

Betrayal   10

Teach them how to love   why should anyone care
    Why should anyone anything   12

Some Florida   13

What Is a Thing   15

Provins   17

Dans le Port d'Amsterdam   19

To Remake It w/ Microtones   21

Le Maître du Désordre   23

Who   25

Secret   27

The Fortune Teller   28

2015   30

POEM   32

County   33

Science Describes Meat   35

Polluted   37

Borgia   38

Micro   40

Why Are You Writing These   41

The Cure   43

Jim Carroll's Ass   45

40 Years Later   46

Speech Isn't Prose, nor Is Thought   48

What Is 'Conscious'   50

Everywhere   52

Before the Cognitive Organization of Matter   54

Lake Failure   56

Berlin 58

Attestation 60

Ladies and Gentlemen 62

I Heard Him 63

It Is the Ascension 65

Pigeon 67

No Longer FBI 69

Change Sound and Syntax a Little Pronoun I 70

Rock 72

Disclaimer to the Urgently Expressive 73

Doug—April 21, 2000 75

The Answer Is Awe 77

I Don't Like This Arrangement 79

Because 81

Safe 83

From Dream Notebook 85

Survive 87

Creating the Memory Collage 89

Presenting Thought   The Old Language   Ocular Migraine Comes 91

*And then again looking for a recent past that is a present thick
with time past and to come so you know what you're
doing in a fact . . . the idea of a spell or hex . . .* 93

Trying to Get to Desert Hole 95

Doug's Prescience of His Death Louise Michel on the Bus 97

Crown and Cancer 99

Dinner at the Prime Minister's 101

Carte de Séjour 103

Breast 105

Uncle 107

Imaginary vs Dreamed 109

A Month Ago 111

As 113

Is It Fibrant or Vibrant Death 115

Sight 117

My Favorite Phrase I Don't Care 119

Dreaming While Awake 120

Anselm Hollo 122

Jimi Hendrix Anecdote 124

These Are the Clothes of Night Woman 126

"I was reflecting the other night meaning

I was being reflected upon that Sheridan Square

is remarkably beautiful . . ."

— "Essay on Style," Frank O'Hara

Preface

I was trying to find out if anything had happened between 2000 and 2017, it was 2017 and I had just finished treatment for my first breast cancer. Did the fact of the cancer have any significance? and something must have happened at some point during those years. I had been sitting in Paris alone since Doug Oliver died in April of the big millennial year—what had been going on? An expanse of timelessness. But importantly it wasn't a chronology, it was actual time, one thing all together. Incidents I remembered emerged on top of those of previous "times"—it was stacked time; friends and relations died and I grieved having known them for so "long." I would get seriously ill, or someone would, was that it, and there was the newsworthy, and I wrote a lot of books. It doesn't matter when except inside the one thought of it. I became more obvious to myself, I discovered I was an unabashed location of unreported events of the Spirit, or Timelessness, the real name of Consciousness. I tried to let as many people as possible into my mind, I changed the past the present and future by blending them. I became the one who held things together as they, the things, kept their motions going, being reflected upon me.

BEING

REFLECTED

UPON

That Kind of Poem

It's lovely no more radiation treatments though ev-
eryone prefers being alarmed about politics
to poetry and that's a mistake   But it's a crisis of
course. I'm so happy not to go to l'Institut Curie
at least for months I dreamed of an empty body
last night a decision as to what necklace should be

put inside it. Last June you knew all this was
coming yes and every day writing poetry creating
the real Real World. I answered the phone to
a telemarketer on Thursday and a voice says in French
'I'm calling on behalf of Monsieur Lorenzo the Medium'
I hung up laughing and thought of Lorenzo Thomas

after he died 2005 I dreamed he burst out of his coffin
in Chicago the Diversey St house where we first bonded '72
he was wearing a shower cap but seemed to be
exhorting me to . . . what? and dust there was
dust on him it was a long time of agos   Vietnam
my brother's just back I said to him

who would have thought the poem says I'd be
still alive and in Paris, France for the health care
this dusty form is my beauty crystal neck-
lace you're smashing Lorenzo great poet who
we were I can't figure what lasts on a tiny
planet of phantasmagoria except one's love

Have you forsythia proven John Forsythe
in the driven to remember rain or snow I'm sinking
syntax by vibe, okay? I'm going to that little theater
in the 16th to see Le Neveu de Rameau it is the year of Diderot
they talk incessantly, right. The neveu is ragged the
"je" figure more together I sit in the corbeil my knees hurt
do you have a
life   if I invent and accordingly by buzzes
how to structure it   don't have to answer
period. All I keep of that experience the métro an
image   métro Ranelagh   Théâtre Ranelagh walk down
a hill I'm bothered staring between buildings at two red lights . . .

that I can have been here at all   Historically when it
evaporates, Paris   who will inspect our earthly ruins?
what in-   telligence might be buzz   So much per-   ceptible
everywhere   will *they* have senses?   This, friends
is a group of created emanations for you to take in
whatever spot you're from   to understand me as I
write as I walk towards light and marquee
Is that why bothered   or was I *interested*   Once there was a reign
of terror   every afternoon   'Why come ye not to court'—John
Skelton? Humans are like embroidery, tears, and insect scurry-
ings but you don't have that to whom I refer my
address   Just another theater another place for made-up stuff

Gravel Ghost or Gravel Gertie

I got the shuttle in Dallas
The man sitting beside me window seat
Slept. He was wearing new spiffy boots
and a sort of combat outfit. Then he woke up
Asked to get out and came back from the restroom
wide awake and talkative—drugs? I remember he
told me he'd been in, no still did work for, the
Special Forces. Had been in Europe just now so
I told him I lived in France and we discussed how
the euro was doing. He said he also worked in Vegas—
where we were headed—as a bodyguard for
Sheldon Adelson. I couldn't remember who
that was. The guy had in fact grown up in Vegas
I'd grown up in Needles. We were flying in
over Lake Mead. I remember because I
just came across a photo of a flower called Gravel
Ghost said to grow near Lake Mead white petals
serrated top edges here photographed as slightly
blurry, ghostly. Going to Needles because
Momma's dying . . . She used to gamble at the
Hotel what was its name, in Henderson where Adelson . . .
The man next to me and I resemblant by coming from
the same desert and knowing Europe . . . I will stay
the night in the DoubleTree . . . the lake is drying up . . .
My brother was in LRR not Special Forces in Nam . . .
I used to be a pacifist but now I'm nothing but soul . . .
Gravel Gertie the bag lady in Dick Tracy was the
local nickname in Needles for Marie my
heroine in my book of poems *Culture of One* . . .
Gravel Ghost you beauty you one-eyed star
Purple verbena everywhere existent and certain yellows
plus Indian paintbrush in Arizona, red . . .

Agamemnon

You may have become too detached
knowing how to do things though
you can't stop   like literacy
those other shoes I haven't worn much
high   Why in that production of
Agamemnon did Cassandra wear
platforms? and something about spit
No reason to accept the story you're

given, right? I went to the play in 2011
The chorus was the same face projected
on a screen numerous times with vocal overlap
I have I have never and I refuse have been to
be in a chorus I cannot be the chorus the com-
munity I reject the concept though
there you are   Prose is when you
say what's approved or condemned

I mean poetry that's really prose and in the
chorus you approve of prose though you
speak poetry unknowingly all your life
At that time I but what? As in
theater the lines invade the actors
you in life cannot resist your lines
Bad poets talk about guilt and you nod
but guilt is inarticulable so the real poet

leaves it out and expresses my anguish at being
in a theater alone speaking French to some-
one who turned out to be English dressed up in
black I remember how to be Cassandra I
remember disliking the mirror-image politics
of disagreement allowing cruelty pretense of
being wronged and you do get it? I don't ever
and don't hit back or click tongue callously

given? was it given can you stop what-
ever no I reenter my apartment do you
and do you win remember the hoax you have ap-
proved I don't approve of anything what
I saw coming was only masses of wrong-
headed traffic air-killing foolish hurrying
home everyone hurrying home from it inside
is nothing changing inside where you are . . . No?

have you changed yourself inside Yes I have
working on it in the most incomprehensible
way the chorus wouldn't what about the spit out of
which spit was created   And then I find I'm
no common humanity good out of focus
the building is old and the play is older by
Seneca whose life moral question she walks
and I walk out of that theater having no more lines

no more chorus the community is a hoax then?

Don't Look At

Don't look at anyone with any words or stories
It's very pale like spit or clear snot
Just happened to be here buzz zzzzing
'There's a reason we love you swirling like
Ghosts around you'   'But I was trying to
Remember the past three thousand years'
Sex concentrates mystery that permeates the uni-
Verse   Are you an audience member now there

Were never and nothing ever   It happened like at
The Bataclan . . . the audience gets shot to pieces
If I can have enough space between thoughts I'll
Find out who I am   But you know and we love
I came to this venue to pay the price didn't you
Or the kosher food store   Shrinking the mind is
Because internet too fast buzz that wasn't what I
Said   It was in the highlands going together

Everyone's moving around like game pieces not
Players really   There Beauty there I'm hoarse
This is how we can   All these loose motives what a
Why I stoppit.   I don't have to offer the thing.
In 1919 my mother was born my mother my grandmother
These people Libby press we know who you are
Reality. I am reality. I call to all you spirits
All you saints to cleanse the minds of my living adjuncts.

Remaking our substance and form

when did I start? about 2009
I will in fact remake you. If I could
have a mythical memory. I wish
some of this art were from another planet
I remember the peaceful wooden Jesuses
show at Cluny from about 1200 French or
Spanish? he just seemed to sleep I had a
black coat as usual. I meet people at
la fontaine de Saint-Michel. I generally don't
think about all this as a pompous
idea because I'm changing it to . . . a porous
unlapidary course, freeing you from
it as it shakes off really your mind.
These bodies, these bodies accustomed
as mine to absorbing human-made shock
in the clothes we wear for it, were you here
on November 13, 2015? I was trying to come back
as if I lived here after twenty-five years
so if terrorists shoot up your neighborhood
destroying 'then' after 'if' and keep walking without a
conclusion in words is there one in bodies is there a
difference is there a difference between anything that
we are? no one's anything I mean, I meant
that asleep I dreamed the real one in its colors
we were a form I saved from death by dismantling
the very idea exclamation point. I can't dis-
cover what I was ever doing. I enter this
apartment and do nothing emblazoned with a ruby.

Archival Quality I Remember

Times when people embody psychic events yours
before your eyes as at the CollecTed publication read-
ing everyone who read enacting my life a dense
and complex dream, like actors. Those who were
still alive; someone like Joe interior his collected
Everything. I'm talking about the play

between present and past, matter and idea at point where
the dissolution of the categories becomes a vision.
That was 2007? but in 1970 on LSD I went to
a benefit to Free Timothy Leary and saw the principals
onstage—variously acting out—Jerry Rubin
Alan Watts Jimi Hendrix—as dream bodies or

actors in a play if you only knew which one. Hendrix
who in my anecdote stared into my LSD grand eyes
was the closest to "natural"—really didn't be-
long at this event nor did I. On LSD you see
the space around people and how they don't know
what they are. This sort of real unreality

like when someone dies or a death is announced
and electrified you turn into another—a body on-
stage in Greek drama barren a stiff dance
you have that mask *on*. The mask that's un-
der the daily one? I like to go to plays since
about 2011 because I seem to have descended further

down where no one can see, the real body
sometimes at art exhibits or in old buildings one
thinks 'this feels like the real' . . . as poetry *is* that.
The part of the Cluny that's Roman ruins maybe
below that. I'm dreaming lately of a house that
never existed, that is mine next to the Alley House

it contains a smooth grey wood-burning stove—
energy. A poem is something you can *have*
you read it and you have it. I remember
springtime in various cities where it existed
a quiet body of ecstasy and underneath you the
observer still the magnetic no one supposed mat-

erial but invisible as the one you are are you
I remember running down the street in Iowa City
barefoot so excited with spring its purposelessness
outside our planet. In 2017, everything at the
same time because the furthest-down body is loose
I know when you act, surrounded by the at-

tention that makes you exist and which when you
go you won't take with you. I live where no one
from your world is and what if I'm making what you
can have—even when you go? because it
knows the air, inscribed on it or spoken in-
to it the real body's texture how spring comes.

Betrayal

I keep going back to that word
the French like it trahison the French are partly me
in micro-particular disposition I sing
I'm most fascinated by metaphysical
betrayal and its off-color quartertones I mean
I mean it   that a bit of matter could humiliate

another like in a beginning when of angels . . .
No I believe they play me like a winning king but
in a future I know already while scourged
I remember when X and Y made Ted miserable
Until he died? before he died? but that's before the
time of these poems of my emplacement in the zeros and later

Do you know that all history's happening at the same time
and see the future if you scry, gross matter   It is 2007
someone dear having died I am on an air-
plane to San Diego and suddenly see blue and orange geo-
metrical formations around the periphery of my vision
both eyes is this part of the poem I'm the singer of

tales of bliss and structure of the universe yet unperceived
Is it built like what I'm talking is it in
fact structured when I write "Voices" Ross, the dear dead
speaks to me in the kitchen to say he's happy the dead are
happy I later believe some are sad sometimes, cyc-
lically until they work it out my poems help them

that my poems help everyone that I am re-
structuring whatever this is that is everything so
that nothing's lost but placed new-pieced into a collage
of the transpired remade into a transcendental *richesse*
opening of graves gold light burst out: Grave of Light
gravid of light Grave Alice and laughing Allegra

ocean of chaos breaks collage of tones you know
and who I was am and will be come back to me
in an enormous betrayal by who once left heaven
all those wanting to be matter my own body
born no one can understand   born no one can com-
prehend how many possibilities we once were be-

fore anyone deceived a rock by breaking it
Ross tell me what   You got it he says and what
you've kept to yourself is cool but the Fibonacci series
being no longer how shall we say these irrelevancies
They slide into the collage I say   Yeah he says
That on the other hand anything will do any glue

Because I was upset at your death mine eyes did break
not into tears but figments colored particles castle bat-
tlements they call them swim before me collapse
I rise again for I am everything participatory in
the earth world's illusions this is an homage to Ross
all that exists communicates cry a little, cry

betrayal that there is dying though death the other breathes

Teach them how to love   why should anyone care
Why should anyone anything

I told her 'I'm frightened'   it was 2:40 a.m.
so we took a walk in the dark this was a dream
when I was little I would wake up scared too
in the next dream no one signed up for my class at Naropa
I am 71 years old teach them how to love
would you take that class what would I say
it has to do with . . . no filters
why would there be is there anything
Love's the only thing I can find what is it it
is the holding together I can't locate a different
thing why do you call it that   No Christian I
heard them singing Jesu meines Lebens Leben
a year ago the soprano wore a green taffeta dress
luxury of love sensations not ready-made
in that Protestant church near the Louvre
the pleasure of a thing is love of it the *luxe*
caring for others or all else is that to be?
so if you in your poem combine that with a modicum
of dross why dross I like the word
I think you should write a poem about tiny atoms of the
self I said no I didn't wicked loving lies
I have nothing to tell anymore I've been on the Cross
a lot lately in an effort to keep space and time con-
nected where I am which might be everywhere
I don't want you to fall apart I love you
what shall we do

Some Florida

It was all done in an instant so how remember
waves of green substance splash when is it before
I'm reading what I'll write this morning
at least in my mind   They are fighting in the parking
lot family fat because I'm just off the plane ob-
serving in Florida remember 'cracker'? But the
mild evening air and when I'm dead I'll just
be deciphering mind code instantaneously aren't
you now   The loud argument delights me though not the guy

who picked me up in Orlando   and I got to jog there
walk over armadillos on the bridge to cottage
do you see the language? it can't be only mammalian
or even animal that pervades and in the green
room who DID this why I did in the en-
tire memory of holding rock together
hydrogen or scales   'did you go in the water?'
I disappear into something   there are forms in in-
visibility   Energy as if already   there what do you
fill with it   I'm seeing hen scratches on a board
You didn't have to go this far becoming god on
a handout   what kind of   there have to be kinds
voice says   I'm always in the big room but I liked
for example going to with women the supermarket
Sky is the emblem of sky   manatees boat and I

come back here I mean Paris this time meaning then
we had a cold summer   if there is only to hold
it all together a linguistic energy say to say our
live dead structure edgeless I wrote this long
ago in a compelling memory moment stretch-
ing can you hear it do you sense the stars it's not
predestination someone says   especially if you don't
perceive what you do so in a line the lines
buzz and move back and forth I was pleased in the

bright rosettes you called me up spell I dreamed
last night they got a grant to go to London and gamble
omit who   O my love I'll tell you all what to do
for the thread-bind invisible from my all-mind even
the rocks held in place by even melting with

What Is a Thing

Of all the things that can go wrong   what is a thing
which ones cause me to see castle-battlement
colored formations on the periphery of my
eyes I'm not telling   but loopy I mean zany
vision's interesting   'what are you thinking about'
different parts or areas of me are thinking
the conscious one that writes
that has to draw from a boundless obscure cache
and one place dreams
and one place sings
without knowing how   this is obvious
what memory are you trying to recover
not re-upholster   evasion I walk into no *near*
an as early as 8th century church rue du Louvre
Saint-Germain-l'Auxerrois
down the street from which a private de-
tective agency advertising itself in neon
Duluc Detective
there's also a shop nearby for model ships EOL Modelisme   I'm
using I use the church
for *For the Ride* a poem still unpublished in 2017
but this is oh 2010   Also Monet's *Water Lilies* other
arrondissement because the micro-bits can come from any-
thing The Glyph I call it holds all in place

we are leaving earth for another dimension
is it too a self area though tremendous full of
imagined and real dead voices characters and my brother
you are all my brother   no Albert is a particular
dead man I am healing every day
each church is built on another older site endless
layering of who you'd know yourself to be
if The Consciousness could be released into
all of it do you *hear* how this is a poem
different from speaking because the micro-
tones sound holy even when humorous

There is construction near the and the
near the and the trees and something yellow
I never go inside them the churches I like to
take energy from the ground or if I'd
enter sit down planting my feet it's some-
thing magnetic in the shadowy parts of air
and nothing happens
except in the poem
which is profoundly scary if you stay

with it what part of the
and the micro-bits of reality swarm and regather
St what of St Chaos I'll collage a typeset
visage would an extraterrestrial have
to communicate with
what
what do you say O tiny bees joined
into a shape for a somehow mien in outer space

the castle battle-
ments note
structural atoms blue and orange-red
usually a visual 'aberration' for half an hour
just like everything else they are
acquired in my 60s or recovered
from anywhere anything everywhere my
personal definition of chaos
'You're supposed to have a life'
I'm supposed to be reinventing Chaos

Provins

Masklike thinking or thinglike but think-
ing might be art   no more accurate than anything
limned words no that thought's a mask but I was going to . . .
that is remember Provins a year and a half ago I hate this line
and everyone's style   Mask press on there are two bomb alerts that
week one at Moulin Rouge when I go to Opta Blanche
and one gare de l'Est is it the day I leave by train just the
Transilien   I wanted to get away did you think that in
words where is a thought parts of 3, 4 words blur wor blu
go by like landscape sudden no-buildings country
you can't get a cab at the gare of my destination
40 min dusty walk uphill drag valise to Ibis
that's near the old medieval ville touristique but
the season's oh stop this describing ever haunted
I'll never forget this nothing that happens
because the old stones have odd feelings or thoughts of their
own and the green-black shadows the leftover age
not the one you were supposed to, it's a form of form
thought entrapped and in the tower and the musée
painting of the trinity a man with three faces the same ones
how many more might light have or properly said
you went there because it called what stop try-
ing or rosewater-flavored fromage blanc after ribs
left left everything's left they left it flee from me
but I'm not where I am anyway listening

as much as that I like walking by the road hot
cross the highway back to motel it's so off-
season   so just off-season   but I have allergy at-
tack on the bed late afternoon what is it graminées
any music too corny any novel I detest the charac-
terization now I'm portraying something try to
get to where I do you *see* it   right now in Paris pouring
the exactness of the dimensions of fate are hegemonic
in spirit vortex some sort of collapse of what you're sup-
posed according to society's and the thought structure but it's

and below what I think towards others are these . . . threads
almost invisible so many seem maze-like but intend-
ed   Nothing you stand for is really there either
the beauty of the but you called it   it wasn't
They have been so late to tell me   'You have been so late to hear'
We didn't flee from you that sometime didn't know how to find thee
Are you masks   Are you they say are you

Dans le Port d'Amsterdam

There are so many places that when you go to them
they're all the same in their difference or people
I will let you come in if I don't have to know you too
much   That's how people like their poems all the same
within the group but what is my topic memory
where the edges change and the form can't drift why
would you remember? too easy   I went to Amsterdam in
2004 and was terrified by the Van Goghs it was cold
Becky and I watched a terrific clip of Sinatra singing Angel Eyes
and smoking   this in the hotel room I only remember
to tell only remember to remember like in another place
getting dressed say, people wear clothes and tell anec-
dotes do I have to   I just crossed something out
like a secret   how important is hiding something
when nothing is important? first I sat in the gare du Nord
huddling I huddled near a little heater Amsterdam
was colder and the crows flew over the field in a painting
that emitted waves of depression and fear but was still beautiful
is this a poem does it create a zone   of cognition that ac-
complishes grace not like a factory but miracle?
you see what I mean that if I just wanted to *remember*
or trauma these words we think mean a complete experience
what's that there were no benches in the Amsterdam station
so hippies couldn't lie on them in a previous era
I returned to Paris and found out I no longer had hepatitis C
I had carried it around for over thirty years without knowing
when I found out was my interpretation of 30 years of
life erased no I didn't have that   I've forgotten a part
about microtones   that what you're hearing in your mind
reading this is bits of confronted life particles or
death particles whichever   I don't know what you
were born for not a proper statement chum
the last time we saw our cat Wystan in 1997 Doug kissed his
ear and said Goodbye Chummie   sometimes I ad-
dress myself to Wystan in my thoughts and say nothing nothing at all
just a microtonal meow? a bit or slat of air like

something the dead would say an empty speech
balloon full of the tiniest perceptions sounding as non-speech
They speak to me and I can't hear   the diamond
store was open remember though it was Sunday and
we looked at diamonds in Amsterdam I was there does
that matter so I would have something to sing
all of these words angel eyes nothing's hidden except one thing

To Remake It w/ Microtones

I'm sending youse a big bouquet of Roses
not being this person think of another
am I or am I not
with you in Rockland . . .

we'll then go to Edinburgh
because I'm reading an Inspector Rebus
there is a tiny coffin the wind sings Marie
I'm wearing it as a talisman
Several times the Russian microtonalist Gubaidulina ex-
plains that she had to look UP
I first met Carl Solomon at the Gotham Book Mart

Or is this 12-tone a dozen the city is
breathtaking but only human
my plan is to stifle my humanity
no one knows what I mean do you Allen
I was not reborn he says your system is
correct and I am here and anywhere

Edinburgh city of humiliation
what would be good for a confessionalist
to say so I could be reviewed in the
New Yorker city of what's that word for what I
free association they said   I am not hu-
man I freely associate raising and lowering
the tone   What are you trying to remember

big black castle paste it on the new collage
'Are these just notes for a poem?' Maria asked of
'A California Girlhood'   I could
say I am now an eschewment
I am remaking even you with the pieces or
are they the firsts the new ones re-
combinatory or their smallest bits
'Are you of your times or one time?'
I will always be with you

Anything I would remember might be
you   even a false one of the Museum of Hearts and
Corpses   I'm taking létrozole for breast cancer
so I'm plugged into the culture nonetheless
I say 'I' so you can understand me
but only I know what I am
at this micropoint in the wind that I am also

Le Maître du Désordre

There's so much I don't need to tell you
the detail is what you say it is I hate that
I'd like to go to the shaman show again how do you
pronounce it I didn't think the curators knew much
I remember the small gooey Legbas covered with muck
Always at crossroads writing about that is that de-
tail it's the click-in of the words together I flew a-
way   I know how to take you through the curtain
I know how to help you die   How can you how do
you . . .   I picked up the skill along the there is no way.
There is no way, anywhere.   Come with me along
the no-way   I can't name anything, from the show
There was a mask that opened into another mask
There was a magic outfit to wear of reindeer
with hood fringe to hide from you my eyes . . .
But, I didn't help Momma, maybe. maybe I did
Not that night at the ER in Bullhead   or maybe
Maybe I did but the details are sacred and vanish . . .

I'm calling to you if you want to come with me
I can break the spell this unreal world holds over you.
I am covered with every detail that's necessary
one thing is an eye and one is a pencil these symbols on
my coat and beads from my beloved mineral world
I'm taking you out of here . . .
there was a place . . . out of here you didn't need sense
possessed by your, finally self you didn't need to catalog
what you considered to have happened
only an idiot believes in the world
Modify nothing ignore what is said
I'm there all the time now   Where? No curtains
You go back and forth it's not so hard
being is simply in touch with each other
You think everybody needs your help alive
you think   think means be   a while

goes by   without drums I was sitting
You might ask for direction or entrance
asking is foolish if you're there
It isn't this world   I'm never in this world when I write but
there's so much I don't need to tell you

Who

It's possible to remember what poems re-
Member for you   Or read them just read them
There's one I haven't read in a long time
That will recall 2005 a hot spring with blue flowers
Though it's a story with characters noirish
A world of micromemories it says I want love

I'm trying for a different
City City Of I could fall down roll down that hill
From Belleville the Belleville of Monsieur Malaussène
You can walk up to l'église Saint-Jean-Baptiste is it
Bookstore Indian resto I haven't in ages
Or will this poem now recall standing with Chris Tysh

Watching women do yoga postures on grass
All over the world   I once walked here with Doug
There's supposed to be a really good restaurant
In 2005 I knew more damage I breathed it in
Recall to me nothing till I know what it's *for*
I could be on another planet a mineral

Their thoughts sparkle net of quiet rigid-
Ity unless you *are* one   it's another speech
If speech means existence and why not
If anything can mean anything Alice we're sunk
I'm changing all that remember?
Remember the franc remember worrying about

Doing the customary correctly not only here
Because I'm not really a human
Shoes why do they wear shoes
Why do they covet each other's whatever
Why do they have to be born why can't they
First be lava then harden   or just assume some particles

Nothing has happened for a long time
Not even something what are you inscribing
Continuous on a stele or what's exhaled try-
Ing too hard to be events that are nameable
Are you with the others come home on the métro
I have to watch over them no matter what

Secret

Something I don't want anyone to know
having naturally secrets where you hid some thing
under the ground, mine from myself   But are they
only linguistic, something you don't tell
what can the poem say for example or not, Jocko
he was a guy in my class. animals flowers and rocks
spoken of by humans as if mysterious
Are you mad at me? I could list them over
the last seventeen . . . years . . . my eyes hurt.
Ruefully   Some people I dislike I don't tell others
about. I didn't tell you I live alone to act crazy
blistering winds of malfortune keep oh keep arising
my thought comes from nowhere my mis-
shapen mind my mind I hardly recognize in its
abnormality   who recognizes, of course. I'm
being secretive, but all of this comes from a void
Everything's a secret and if you know so
you can act. The blank thought behind all the rules
you don't let yourself know you follow.
You don't want me particularly; I could ap-
prove of your magisterial complicity in how
"we" "do" "things"   Convince me that you secretly . . .
the throes of opportunity . . . complots . . . secretly
And now I would confess some "weakness"
My problem with the confessional: I'm not a
Catholic   took it with her to the grave. Grave Alice
My secret is that I'm in complete control of my-
self; no matter how it seems; and how I do it, is a secret.

The Fortune Teller

you have no body even when it hurts so much
some matter has arranged to be you hasn't it
then you go to the fortune teller I went to sev-
eral when young one even had a membrane over
her iris but they didn't understand me as
well as I did   oh I was just curious   Remember

'signs'   what remember   I remember my imag-
ination houses I visit nonexistent or a grotto   no
remember when Joanne got me to write a collaborative
note with her and leave it in a tree for Donald Allen who
was feeling bad   we rolled it up a scroll tied with ribbon
mostly she made me shy at some point I re-

alized, though, she liked human niceness more than I
—the scroll—she liked surprise birthday parties
what I liked was her voice I never knew what
she and Bob Creeley were going on about I was 25
later she said everyone in Bolinas loved me
I know that isn't true and Philip loved her so much

did she really not know that? 'batty inexor-
able logic'   I've said all these things before
Like when suddenly her aesthetic was chang-
ing from Duncanism and Ted wanted her
for the New York School   some part of her
joined it remaining Joanne   but I remember that

moment when Ted, Bob, and Tom Clark all seemed
to be courting her aesthetically   she had such
brilliance and one wanted her to write like one
she would always follow her voice—and Lewis Warsh
'she's becoming more autobiographical'—no she wasn't
she was doing mind/nature/voice partic-

ular to person/life finds expression as 'that flicker'
bird as mind of no-god drifting coastal moment
You were so beautiful   and I'm remembering how
right before Ted died he placed new books on shelf
by bed, by Joanne, Joe Ceravolo, and Anselm Hollo and said
'I have a generation'   b. 1934   I'm sorry I'm just crying

I.M. JOANNE KYGER

if people are animals who can speak
or animals are people who can't

I was tired both of being articulate
and of being an animal   there's mind-speech
the art all an art. I walked out barefoot
on the ice in my dream to label the trees
this would be so much more for every word's a
universe or thee. That my memory I can't lose

because it makes real the whatever to exist
my memory becomes you. Moonlight becomes you
one of the trees was called Wenceslas
I have been trying to remember who I was
before 1945 year I was born I have given
up on the world of things. I give up on your
house and clothes   your heart and your smelly autos
But elsewhere before I was born I am still alive.

An example of what I do in life 'try to remember'
In the dream the ice wasn't cold but was ice
And eat this beige food in strips the same said
Before I was born I didn't eat   perhaps conveyed to
you the thoughts so particularly expressed as to be
changeable particulates a poem that mutates in
minute sparkles   Does this one? I
was that anyway. Whatever I'm going to

write down I've already written chang-
ing it as I go the bits of thought mica chips
but moving unlike ice   we stood on the ice
together I have led you here to remake the uni-
verse entirely since it's a product of your im-
agination. The other animals are happier than
we are don't try to change them together in litters
Darkly shown the moon that night of the abstract frost

My thoughts said that we were larval fashioning
kiosks of news   No they said the hard underfoot
kept not being cold because its qualities had been
badly named   and you might be a deer thinking 'ree'
But never born I was always there with all capacity
To communicate the everywhere thought   I stand
before the board on which my poem al-
ready exists, changing slightly as I think it

I write it I think it there is no writing before
birth instead there is everything   On the ice an
alder hasn't been named nor a blackbird
nothing happened that wasn't this glittering
freedom of movement kind of sound if there were
no senses keep saying the primal substance
the ones of it where there is no size and no one
You remember and forget what will happen its use

is there that I used life to understand death didn't I

POEM

It doesn't matter if a poem is clear or not
hard or not   It's basic and ongoing creation
of the universe in terms of its particles as I speak
it the poem   If you're reading it you hear me too
the bits of sound thought word seen, without senses
if you're dead   All you have to do with it is nothing
Everything else is such a big deal thing   poetry's
mere reality   No proof just be here   Proving's
a human invention poetry is what you do with
mind which is what there is   just listen a little.
No one cares if you understand it   who understands
why we're alive   I haven't understood any-
thing since . . . an academic subject I was walk-
ing say near the Grands Magasins—How? you once
learned you learned how to walk the man
with the monkey and three dogs isn't there anymore.
I go inside and buy presents Baccarat or Swarovski
I understand death now.
                              A crazed taxi driver
told me he did time for protesting war in front of
Galeries Lafayette   is this part of the poem I gave up
and just listened to him   for which audience he was so
grateful he carried my suitcase to my door   in Decem-
ber when I had had surgery but not yet radiotherapy
He was from La Réunion and it is possible,
holding it together, with what are called words
but again particles of communication thee particles
all that's there?   all that's there.

County

I'm staring at end of bed San Bernardino County
blanket draped   I grew up in that county
now I'm too old to have done that or too far away
inside the microparticles the memory glue of you
The last time I went there Momma's funeral
Then that summer in Needles hottest rain ever recorded
In 2015 the San Bernardino terrorist massacre those

convex faces in their US Border Patrol photo
I am always so sick trying to accommodate what you
do   What do I remember Xmas 2015 everyone al-
ready sad here from Nov 13 attentats   and those that
the whole Arab world endures the poem coheres
the one you didn't want you say was she too
rich for heartbreak or she too successful

I didn't know something what was it how to be
popular I'd tried not to since I discovered you had to
kill at least figuratively   you might wish an
entire race dead or pity another every day
'she is using it'   high above and maybe above
you I hear the tones whir change   what's hate
something that feels really good I've been told

wear shades wear a mask or cloth over-face who
a Venetian when the play starts to protect you
from scrutiny for what purpose at perpetual
carnival a lit crit favorite   don't enter he says I'm
cleaning up now I realize I didn't properly I say
fill out the application for the T. S. Eliot Prize
now it's too late in my life in a popular quartier

Yet I'm dreaming of you O memory
how you protect from dissolution the stars any kind
if I could only know what really happened

I had to she says the terrorist by my logic what
else is there   the memory that love is I say
that I will give you anyway all there is being
intermixture but the greatest of these isn't faith but illogical charity

Science Describes Meat

I however you see it torn festering but those aren't
I wasn't words. Conveyed by machine in the morning
you go to Prague, say   bar plays Rolling Stones all day
In this particular hotel on the square the wi-fi only works down-
stairs. Trevor will go to and the names don't
come fast, where Desnos died, Terezín Theresienstadt con-
centration camp. I feel surrounded by war dead every
day I'm there tourists buy garnets I do
and antique ruby earrings with gold I am wearing you souls
and give a talk on Charles Olson. What do you hope for now?
You can cross the river don't remember if I do the
Jewish Cemetery's closed cold in May I ate
a burrito I found a bookstore with French books
There didn't have to be such a thing as hope defined
I wouldn't have thought of it   myself and the dead of Prague
tell me they find the conception grotesque   they
still feel terrible   where did abstract words come
from? but I asked what do I   'what can I hope for' sung
I'm concluding that I never hope. Bob Hope left
in my ancient dream, the shack where I was shaman
Bring the dead home, bring them if they're not
home for I'm somehow home the needs-no-hope
And I take them on. Black garnet pendant
I met some real people, Sam, Susana, Olga, Louis—
the names associate by esses and els don't they
I heard a Norwegian conceptualist read and I
I confronted such hurt near that arch
hurt bent back and in into one and down it
could hardly get up how could it be led
There must be in mind another place and eventually
eventually must be now   Joel's father said
he was happy   to be in America after Auschwitz
But thou the dead that there   and that this species in
its imagination, that it can make imagination in which
this is a *thing* is *this* a *thing* and if it *hurts* I
will make you sing with the hurt of the actual *nerve*

in *my* fantasy . . . Did we make ourselves? did we?
I am going to lead you from what we made from
the mind we made for I'm changing the matter its atoms
I insist on taking you home this is no fantasy
because you're there now and we're just there

Polluted

it's so polluted   so more and more polluted and
hot   Remember the year 2006 it was in the '70s
at my birthday in November   we saw a flock of parakeets
like green pigeons in a tree in Brooklyn
there was a botanica in that neighborhood
I wondered if you could buy a goat there to sacrifice
a fantasy of propitiation to the Yoruba pantheon
there are no gods there are no people the words are lies

if we called the gods people and the people gods . . .
would we act like adults would we not stab
the mammal to see if it bled   I once saw a guy
who'd just been knifed on the corner of 1st and 9th
I was a block away he was bleeding I heard sirens
then I can't remember   the washing machine
the lavage it's clean and I don't know if he lived
that was earlier when I used to know how to remember

I am holding you together   I am like Legba
and I understand crossroads as every moment
I was living in Paris but traveled often to New York
at the corner of France and US who are you it
doesn't matter   as long as I can find the ally
in myself a light bursting out of my forehead and heart
I am standing here hoping to appease your brutality
words said in the daily way not poems are incorrect

though an anecdote might be true and art
but the sun doesn't care about us and we just try
to get by still owning cars like suicidal idiots
I just crossed out lines about watching a film with Eddie
ancient Village folksingers remembering Dylan
I remember Mississippi John Hurt at the Bitter End
I could say or who got rich and famous what was that
all about   I *am* the crossroads what's happening

I'm what's happening porous and permeated with scorching light

Borgia

her father is the pope you get it the pope
has three children she has a baby with one of
her brothers that part's not historically accurate
there's a lot of poisoning   also not verified by
research honestly I don't believe anything
I haven't witnessed myself and what I saw
was an enormous beautiful powerful manip-
ulation of the voice and language by Hugo and the Comédie
art seems the only real argument for natural
selection   but we can't ask the other species what

they appreciate I am always walking out to meet you
you will tell me some political silliness
you believe the media   you who have never known a
politician   don't believe righteous speech in any year
in oh 2010   but if you were married to a creepy doddering
duke   that year I'm still visiting Needles and my
mother whatever we say to each other tissued
into motion about the house and town do you want
to go to Laughlin and play the slots translates to
let's go up the river   it's a dance between her and my aunt

all day they pretend they might not and then they do . . .

Elsa Lepoivre's voice as Lucrèce obliterates Needles she
and the duc when he counters her my pen's going here's another
forcing her with words his diatribe after hers to
his will   have you ever seen physical force used no not
myself though it's implied in all we do if you
and if you then and if you don't pay, out on the side-
walk say they are cop-backed the year I dream
that, though I live in Paris, I'm cast outside on St. Marks Place
or boxes full of my manuscripts are I have always felt evictable

is that a metaphor like 'layered with conviction'
the bell rings Alice is ready   it was the speech caught

in the throat let out in air or on paper even
that I am gambling on, say I stopped hav-
ing the wherewithal to gamble but money isn't durable
the glue is words and she asked me in the parking lot at
Basha's about changes in her will in re the executor-
ship though it wouldn't be much   it wasn't
under the trees to the side   nothing's true I thought dur-
ing the play nothing about the world anyone says

I am a sayer and I don't believe   it is a fabric of saying
as you breathe   none of our customs don't finish that
across from the Needles cemetery where we all are
yet she was kind and interesting peaceful to be with   words
true is that true   in 2010 at a future will I not
see these mountains again full of sky towards Kingman
yes and that's now   some Lucrèce Borgia really lived
is corruption a concept does anything you do
happen reverberating farther out to possible simil-
ar structure of so-called matter   or didn't do a thing

Micro

if there was no definition as if you were born
in an exact way to achieve dust
then I am free before birth grand but
do I have to find you? you left me I say
though I left the country as if there were that
for another you all left me at the beginning

to be brats in stasis pretending evolution or even drastic
change who has ever changed   'it's just these details
a faint drum no one in outer space hears' I went to the zoo
and saw myself you say   I can't finish these poems ever
I say I still don't know what I "did" for 16, 17 years
I once came to this planet   I never learned the language

I and no consequences as of my actions for I couldn't find
a line   finally I don't accept you   it's too uncomfort-
able anywhere but before birth I wouldn't have so
trivially so maddeningly had to define
it's crazy here but I wouldn't have known 'crazy'
and actually I don't I don't know who you are and who

I've presented to you all these years is a lie
a lie among words for oneself though I
know now who I am a what is that word an
apostate   have I misspelled it   I am god
I am the state of being among states
I am memory of the present the only one that remembers it

if you want to come along okay   I don't take prisoners
do you understand now what you've been told not to know
the connection it could be called   I have to get back
to before to where it's the apparent and might be words
if they're it fibrous shiny and all the other stuff
can't you sense it you this mind that hums

Why Are You Writing These

to try to remember
what you is that nothing much happens for
17 years it was rich
living in isolation in a populous city
remember when I hated my neighbor because he was noisy
I didn't hate him I couldn't look at him I wanted to
kick him out   he held raves every weekend
I called the cops a lot and worked with a certain policeman
who discovered my neighbor had been arrested in Bordeaux
for breaking furniture   he finally stopped paying rent
had to leave then the gardienne and I gave thumbs-up signs
across rue des Messageries   she has since moved to Valencia
I'm interested in how totally against him I was
you could say I have sensitive ears that simply react
his mother came up from Toulouse once to help him clean
we were overrun with mice she caught seven
one morning with glue traps excuse me she said I'm the mother of
your neighbor who's sometimes noisy do you have mice
I tried to tell her I'd seen them slide down the gas-pole like firemen
but I didn't have the French for that and French firemen don't
she had a dream of moving to San Diego

I don't mind any of it except for my ears
I was born receptive and sound shakes me up
I have a poem in which the universe is like a vocal cord
it must also be an ear infinite reception
music destroys thought poetry is it I couldn't have
been bothered to tell this story in prose   A decision was
taken after time began to maintain a prose universe
I have been bored ever since and keep to myself
though contrarily trying to save you from the materials
of your destructive lives masses of noise anything
to forget what and maybe I am only a nerve
or am nerve if you could remember shut up and remember
or is it not remember I am in a state of vibration

every possible sound available why or is it only
something to do the one thing to do or is it only
Helen Morgan again singing Why was I born / Why am I living
I have nothing to show for my time but poems
what do you have

The Cure

You start and then you make rules for yourself grad-
ually   It is predicament same how to live but
why   Animal habitudes so complex or am I an un-
inherited mind that obeys no rules of my species
I perhaps speak as a badger or stork and if I am
granite I've gathered my mien together over mil-

lennia my mien and adamantine depth
the spars and no junk   Keep portraying something
I just don't want to in 2003 I am diagnosed
with hepatitis C and write In the Pines and coedit intro-
duce and annotate The Collected Poems of Ted Berrigan
the treatment legendarily grueling strips me of weight

and moral confidence my liver is scarred but do I have
that or anything? I perhaps speak as a bat
wolf bear or owl with its terrifying howl
in the forest wild and drear   It's connected by song too
I can see the atoms singing to each other can't you
I was welcomed into the French community of medical patients

in which you're treated regardless of worth monetary
or social   they treated me and I wasn't pretty jolie ou
Française   What is being sung the song of your location
as physical one whose molecules observable co-
here can you hear them   I told the story of myself as folk
and vibrated to Leadbelly and Man in the Long Black Coat—

I had often worn one myself Blind Willie McTell and
Careless Love the species motto   I am watching the elec-
tion I mean now but politics being shitty species be-
havior of competition domination and looking for ex-
cuse to hate and beat up *so don't do it* (a line from
the theme song of Baretta) it's been It Was Just One

Of Those Things in my head in the kitchen mornings recently
also I'm wild again beguiled again et cetera
We saw an emu with its head holes staring at us
in a zoo last week American culture now figures nearly naked
women singing songs they wrote too   the turtles' heads pointed
all in one direction this is how crazy you caused me

how crazy you caused me. You caused me to leave
my home everyone causing everyone every
thing. None of these folk beg forgiveness for
being like they are material fools. I was the soul
of it   You forgot how to hear my whispers
deaf as posts. Wood the tribe of wood that is

I would have blood taken I was tested
was anemic had rashes and pondered my interferon-
caused depression pitying my doctor during
the gross global-warming-caused canicule of '03
she couldn't take the heat like me   I carried a chilled
injectable dose to Chicago so I could read poetry

and met Mrs. Green a housekeeper at the U of C faculty club
who placed her hand on my heart and prayed to
Jesus for my recovery one of the genuine thrills of those years
I assured her she probably *wasn't* suffering a
recurrence of her cancer (last time I was there still
alive had retired)   A Parisian acolyte of a guérisseur

had also in her boutique suddenly put her hand even
fist against my heart   they were worried   people
love each other don't they don't they
and the animals we disrupt so huddle flesh to flesh
It can't be right, how we do things.
So I could see better I became myopic as a child

Fiddling with the particles of your soul. The wind
as adviser or I accept none. Nothing but a cure.

Jim Carroll's Ass

Nothing seems real   yet I'm willing
to play 'the real' game for ones I love
and when I'm sick I go get pills
but more and more hovering above it I'm
and then is it a question of for who that's why
I no longer have memories I don't care about them
though I can contrive more but I don't
belong in them anymore   'Do you really think

everyone is benighted?' someone in effect asked
I guess I said yes   what emanates from me
is crackling love electrical currents an aliveness
everything else I do remember playing games
Pac-Man at midnight in the months before Ted died
Jim Carroll's favorite being Ms. Pac-Man
one has an official position that humanity's history
has erroneously deemed women untalented

ineffectual at its projects over literally millions
of years therefore humanity's likely to be 'wrong'
about anything no everything and nothing what-
soever is happening except for pain isn't this
ridiculous yet I like to remember Jim Carroll
mooning Ted at the entrance to Julian's Billiard Academy
the first time I met him he was showing off for me
and had a pearly ass this is cerebrality

but not within the time frame of my research
Somewhere in a room outside this whole place earth
an infinitely large unshaped one
this poem already written is being translated
through tubes or pathways into my mind or heart
I am and it's all covered   by me who already wrote it
I don't have an audience we are a membrane of re-
ceptive contiguity abstract abstractly avial and wing-white

I.M. JIM CARROLL

45

40 Years Later

I went there to see the Cornells
can't remember a single one   in order
to think about   how to reassemble the new
universe from its old pieces I'm not kidding.
Either to or from the Art Institute young Somali cabbie
who innocently used the word 'fucking' as an adverb repeatedly
while he spoke casually to me had picked it
up as sound without meaning and was rather sweet.

They were all on the wall together
I gravitate towards ones with sky maps marine blue
I exemplify gravity and you are drawn towards
what I see like my room I'm already in
but in the new one only gravity itself transparent as some
saran wrap green chair brown chair broken
because I once threw it across the room mad at someone
in the new universe I am not a creature,

a bird is not dead, a woman is not young
a memory is not forced or prefabricated,
one's thoughts too are a force field, and the colors
don't care what they are next to. I was in Chicago
staying at the Godfrey Hotel and kept standing on a
certain corner   or in the other direction an underpass
some rhyme no reason if you live that long or forever—
all the naughty things Rudy said about Cornell.

It was one that reminded me of my frequent dreams of
skies with unseen-before uncharted mutable
constellations   I've never known where I was going
I am here. The dead planet still glued together
but one component of this mind that
if all the components of senses float in it
and emotions then I am a pre-Socratic original or
vaster the container   Can't you hear me calling

will there always be another object
will you always live around the corner from an Hôtel du Nord
(at the gare du Nord this morning the police sought Three Dangerous
Men)   Will qualified as a danger something float out, float out
and adhere   with a sea-creature ballerina skirt
quiver signal that it is the Utopian and I am becoming ex-
tinct because I won't pay admission at the entrance
to 1000 BC or 2015 AD because
in the new outer space you can't make me

(that was an old broken window storefront
worn heavens behind   layer after layer)
How you renew is with a moist transparent spirit
or How you renew is by mixing negativity with light
until the medium or substance of us is refashioned to
include "evil" so no one's left out
They hadn't heard of us in the Andromeda galaxy
Will I always have heard of us or evil I don't know

Speech Isn't Prose, nor Is Thought

I'm sorry my mother said in a dream Everyone
should have a house and enough to get by.
I have a couple of rooms and dream only literally
of owning a detached structure 'then you'd have a car
somewhere' how the planet is practically dead
I can barely get out of bed today much less maintain
them   It's these pills I say to anyone   Last night

I dreamed I collected objects a little like Fabergé eggs
and sold them to a Bob-Wilson-like gay collector
This you have done   he was training me I lost some
and couldn't keep track of which ones he wanted
because it's all invented not shelter and food you'd say
shelter is and the first amoeba ate what
the air is placid on election day unknowing

or the day of the death of the one that you
I didn't make it or I did I didn't have to
in the last 17 years I knew how to love though
but that wasn't it for I live in the universe
and am its own house   denying all your local cust-
oms if I can keep my joints together
not to speak of the name of your job or forever as

you'd think   I'd lost one of the eggs a blue and gold
Make of it what you will   the human motto
any old business   I don't need corroboration oh
and if I die who you ignore for a rabid mythology
as you your fictions make of the group or one or currency
you will say to collect us and smother the science of thinking
though I'll think anyway and escape your cutting edge

I walked for 17 years down the rue of message boards
the boulevard of broken the treaty of versus I and I
ignored the worldly stable of schoolboys and girls
bullies and criticists you don't have to be so

you don't really have to have a government
drifting away along the path of the milky way do you
really think we're accidents of matter that

must be organized? and if you do are the victims
of "matter" "must" and "organized" unknowing for a fact
any time I'm not part of it I'm rejoicing
I walk down bd Haussmann or Second Avenue
I walk where in no time flat particles of spirit
you want to mask with your words of anti-bliss
I can't take it anymore to be structured

and restructured modeled and cured told and deciphered
I am indecipherable I walk down
and in a nether-room preach to all the souls there are
that there's no culmination and the nothing goldly glistens
you don't exist as this I was sick from your noise and pain
your very matter so walk with me down rue true danger
dare it leave your religion of going on at any cost

as if they would kill you if you didn't they are you

What Is 'Conscious'

I just had the most awful dream
that there were two swimming pools indoors
and in one my baby was suddenly bloodied then disappeared
I looked for the baby in both pools we were all in bathing suits
couldn't find and then suddenly the lifeguard a man wear-
ing glasses on his high seat said his daughter was sorry if
she . . . there had been something not really linearly
but in the way of dreams integral   and I said

'You're telling me in front of all these people—you the universe
are telling me my baby died'   'You mean
you didn't know'   'Doesn't matter   It's the only thing here'
I wake up crying.   And isn't it the only thing here?
On the previous page of dream book I see I've written

'the monkey is dying
Allen, Doug
Mts with trees
the three bloodied men get back up
one now without a hand
follow me all day, bother me I say to dead Syrians
I'm trying to change the composition of the universe'

The lifeguard resembled Remington P. Patterson—
practically RIP—my teacher at Barnard of
Elizabethan and Jacobean drama the bloodiest fucking
literature in the world   I don't know
who these people are   I am so trapped bodily
I recently thought call the mind the body
and the body the mind? no it was more like
call gravity mind and mind gravity

anything any other scenario
as long as the baby doesn't have to die
in the primal pool   if you say this is raw
I reply by whose rules   by whose definition of life

are you asking what poetry is and if it's of use?
nothing's of use! But I'm just babbling because
someone died the first time and a man on a throne
apologized   no one's well guarded, of course

I've always said don't follow me
now I frankly think that you should
otherwise you won't know when I've changed it
it's all in flux right now renameable
whatever you do it's your mind holding
matter which is mental in place that's
shifting as you see it with your brain of stars
shattering its name and furniture

None of the governments are here   your
ideas and theirs blood external the hoax
of coagulation I call it rampant
Some joker's playing his popular music again
Let it all happen collapse and fly out of your-
selves the only sticking together's of the mole-
cules of soul to tell each other we ex-

ist that's all the universe is vanity

Everywhere

That my mind didn't belong to my head as con-
tainer as if it could be so localized
but was everywhere or anywhere obviously
I perceived the other day in the métro or maybe my bed
there was really nothing being me that way
though I was thinking hard and wondering how to

express this thought   nevertheless to you
where I am   or where am I   is it mine
how large is it   Les arènes de Lutèce come to mind (do
I mean mind) I'm in 2011 trying to be of Paris

beginning to write some Thing out of knowing I live
in an area once home to lepers and prostitutes where is my
folder of maps and facts   near the old hôpital Saint-
Lazare or medievally earlier I breathe afloat
create a group of characters like disciples of moi-même
the mind behind the facade of the rue de Chabrol

in an unpublished book *Our Voice: A Bible* the voice and mind be-
ing the same I turn on the fan to drown out the
music of my latest noisy neighbor I make my own
mentally can you hear it   There was a poem that'd get written

at Iowa with wonderful opening lines followed by a clutch
a getting lost for lack of actual mental process though
would sound right in the end with that ending sound
I saw some of such poems in whose book recently
there it is I thought he didn't get middles which are everything
though it's better than an overall sleek-machine poem

in the arènes but I walked a path around and orange flowers
to remember the Romans were here way before the wall
of Philippe Auguste   fragments of which are on that street
where I've read my poetry rue Tiquetonne Quo Vadis

in your supposed body my mind wanders out to
bd Magenta remembering pages I cut and still
feel attached to there were ghosts around a phantom
fire and we told each other from different eras how
to love including the 13th century raped and murdered
girl who speaks through cut throat protesting

we banished her equally dead assassin from our com-
pany all my thoughts go out to you too
has there been a story does your suffering
float or did you suffer have you forgotten the middle parts

that everything is outside us a common mind
it's there if you go to it you can have mine it
didn't start with my birth the prostitute who'd died with
dementia now knows   she said that what she
wanted when she was alive was only to sit and think
these were my people that year and what you

need to know about a poem is that it can modulate
changing keys the song in your head might
your head might you know   even without the written
word   just let go of it

Before the Cognitive Organization of Matter

I was there after some blowout of creation you swim or float
A few years ago I dreamed I was in the Needles swimming pool
old one   and Greg Peterson suddenly popped up out of water
in front of me but this had once happened   I dreamed an exact
memory of what I had forgotten same mind this connection
to the dream of being speck floating in purple primal sea—
I feel he has always been with me though dead since forty
and certain others from school   You walk to the pool without shoes

from bush shadow to telephone pole shadow to further bush
I'm back facing mountains the whole Colorado River valley
After my mother died and I'd left for the last time dream
I am naked to waist climbing up from the gully (mountains would be
     behind me)
pulling myself up but pressing self skin against desert earth
Meanwhile or then in Paris what about the beginning:
it is said nothing was stable it was violent—words
that stable's different from a moving composition you don't recognize

though your consciousness is somehow the judge already
things I've said for the last seven years events of my
life the earth is so *used*   and nothing can be *new* but
the Mojave had remained primal you could get lost in
a few square miles of it, know what I mean?
And die of exposure why not I had a friend (not Greg) who did
had accidentally shot and killed someone and in guilt
went out in summer away from town to sit

in full lotus position until he died they found him that
way my brother told me   I kept going back where else
would I go but came home to Paris my forty-four
square meters 'Your building's a slum' my friend Erika said
Before the cognitive organization of matter it was
my mind   and I projected my body or image into it,
choosing my parents who also chose me
Paris (trope) is weary with species history dirty beneath

the bâtiment souls arise from it demanding poems
finding me from earth or air which are nothing to them
'If you hadn't become such a crank . . .'   And the wind
cries Immortality   it's a little planet I've said that and not
that grand a universe   unless you include its involutions in-
finite of thought and inside one that infinity
where do thoughts come from coursing
from beyond the Seven-Mile Mountains or from everywhere inside

Lake Failure

In Lake Failure   that's funny a handful of years when
the idea of failure   and I thought, I haven't failed I don't
an example of just a word. I was shining be-
cause I didn't care now there was no expert
except me in the area of how to live. Or write
I still wanted an audience I like that word

hearing the cosmos a daisy no hearing the
involute the imbricated layers of expression
vintage flowers   It's that I wasn't anything and didn't
have anything. A definition of holy maybe
You can go there and see it occasionally   Old shoes
of a medieval person or a used crown small

a list on a page, Radegonde's signet ring
an unusually lively calligraphy with colors and birds
How did one talk without the alphabet and will I
learn how again ever I can't go on this a-way
can't I say them just say them   I heard a black-
bird last week singing the most fantastical things

'this is my accumulated experience of time and place'
I felt I was walking with Jimmy this morning
wrong country right soul   Foggy rain for two days
the petals get ragged, white and the center loses bitty
parts on bent stem end pink sprays straight ahead
I'm allergic now to everything I see

wanted to touch me. I could touch you or air
the muguet on every street corner or bouche de métro
we're an implication of a silent texture
or do I mean unseen   that
if I don't speak every day as is often the case what
I write in my own language radiating

I am now the only source of. Influences moot.
Maps of how to go on a pilgrimage don't
quite work. Then they found St. Anselm's foot
and encased it in silver. I am certainly a relic
Touch any gemstone to get better you know the
names cinnabar malachite chalcedony Salome-Where-She-Danced

if I were just thinking it with in other words
a magnetic force to its parts of obligation
like parts of speech a loosely bound wind
don't crank it up. I wasn't it and didn't have it
for earth years I said it to the other parts
of this out-of-scale world neither large nor small nor medium

Berlin

You have an impression of trees
trees and flowers I'm now allergic to too bad lilacs
no pollen in desert childhood
as if extraterrestrial I survey the pleasures
of parks dining the competition for any-
thing not because you need it I or you
did I try to run the table pool-hall expression
I will pressure you to do better   oh? do?

this is a time of no it isn't or era or age of no
this is a mishmash of possible fool details
from where I am if I die of it I can always be dead
pity and compassion still disgust me though love doesn't
I mean right now and 'the age of' falls apart
I like to sit on a park bench with other poets
allergic to birch oak and graminées
telling the folk gossip of our repeated breaths:

'after you've gone' sing it you can talk about me too
I mean I've gone the wind broth another
phrase like 'collective failure' two shades of lilac
darker and lighter now wouldn't that frost your
and the bordelaise grape crop bad we were talking of A.
A. J. and also W. and maybe D. on the level of 'it's only
words'   how else would I know anything
smell it and eat a giant schnitzel forego the schnapps

now back there is a new president not me
will I dream of him signifying the present
you have nothing to complain of you say
it is a lover's right the plaint the regrets the loss of
that I did that or anything 15 mai a computer
virus rampant that is it's imaginary
oh the sick patients the French cars oh the badness
of the bad bad poverty racist degenerate fore-

closure licensing executive the scandal of
the anthropocene hagiographic death trip
rock stars whoever's rich and famous ass-kissed
I was watching my life become a traditional story
'Do you mind?' are there really only people
is there really only here? I don't think so
I'm not sure I have to care about what happened to me
I'm trying to convince you of something life on Mars

Attestation

Okay. She was diagnosed with cancer Nov 2011 I'm al-
ready in the States giving readings   suddenly I'm flying to Vegas
she has had surgery there and is in a rehab, temporarily
I can see her eyelids with eye open for the first time in my life—she
and most of her siblings have the epicanthic fold   she's changed she's dying
a nurse practitioner gives her six weeks to two months to live
(she has a lovely nurse named Valery who wants a poem
dedicated to herself)   And there's a dog they bring around
for cheer. I can't write this way in sequence it surrounds me in its parts

she goes back to Needles; eventually dies in Bullhead; I
fly back and forth, sisters aunt others are often present

Let the steles in the overlife record
that I can't go back there now that's one
or that I'm outside the house a bird in the back-
yard at night. Because I'm in Paris and she's dying
in the house I mostly grew up in, project myself back one
night in December   did you did you really? I
answer do you know that American politics has become
a fantasy?   All I can think of is that I thought I did
I know that backyard I'm at the window or near the fence
she doesn't want me there because I know she's dying
others don't seem to   then she wants me there again
and I'm there and back here and there and then there again.
I hate people who listen to music on machines
it's a true hatred   I can or can't write this
the idiot in the courtyard the blam blam rock
beat for those who won't face up to living
                                        She got
smaller she stopped eating expecting to get well
is dying getting well maybe   I hate hate his
music I found two versions of the song Tabu and
played them for her, by the Lecuona Cuban Boys and by Xavier Cugat
Slowly I will cause his machine to shatter will I . . .
he stopped . . . My mother finally started hallucin-

ating but not much . . . he started a new vibration and
thump   She had to go to Bullhead to die I've
written elsewhere a roadrunner and scorpion were there
She had convulsions and forgot why she was hospitalized
I told her: I was being used for most communication
purposes especially the more brutal
ones this is what I do isn't it   stopped
and if you use me you   use me and get mad at me for it
it was nonetheless a peaceful careful dying.
The details are, it's these non-entities   but chosen to be
remarked upon as if a life doesn't continue
anyone knows it does and there's a further consciousness
the so-called parts become a re-arrangement
in the ulterior reality, that too you can know here, but in the ulterior
or superior the selection and flow continue
unmechanistically the current interpret-
ation's atrocious she is staring at me with
her lit-up smile and glasses por favor and laughing
es su madre, me gusta mucho her terrible border Spanish
of a person without bounds

Ladies and Gentlemen

I do not earthquake follow your attention
is there anything to see black and white filmed high-
way or collapsed extraterrestrial collection of triangles
the threat of god that is me is to grow a new talent
I am making it   every dream was my own
choice   where in there? do you care
if you have a human form? or form? Inside from where
you speak I am first speak in no language

phosphorescent I am trying out to name the holy particle
gold one   please no hoax please I say
child runs into darkness I particle the I-particle
will not pronounce you dead. It floats up from
where sit and has its own choice   broke open over the land
I project that you are not damned
it is another consciousness and doesn't wear
speaking for it all   no one can get past me

don't let it break up I don't serve your event
the interpretation said to be my form
I saw what your form that I inhabit
is thought to be   but I see it differently
and what I do with it now will change everything
rising up from the apportioning of species
to follow I-particles in the night
I'm resisting how they entrapped my shoulders

follow me now the I-particles escape every-
where the floating or zooming sparklets
there's no aim   and to comprehend it wasn't a life
to die from   it was language   speak this one
every dream is your own choice you chose it in the dark

I Heard Him

I heard him talk to me in my mind and tell me what to do
which I did and he was right, though dead   I wrote to her
and she needed me to   the thing is, I heard myself
talk to him   without control didn't know that I'd say it
I said You   he said Yes   he said It's for Albert   Now
the I that said "You" was not the one I was going
along with in the daily way getting ready to unlock
my door "I" didn't know anyone was there and sud-
denly my "own" mental voice said "You!"   Further-
more he replied in *my* voice   was using my voice

in my head. This was about 2009 I've become another
I know what I know you say   I know al-
most everything I don't know why we have to live
this I'm not even sure we're really participating
in. Do you think dreams are slipped into us by . . .
I like to run because it isn't like moving so
reminds me of dreams a man's making friends
with a heron in the pond at les Buttes-Chaumont
photographing him this morning   But he's mine,
my heron! discreetly I don't tell him but I may

the heron came towards me once. Almost left the water
But I didn't notice soon enough and couldn't stop
moving that way when you run   in the same park
since 1995 remember the flasher the first one
I've seen several   different countries and races
same preoccupation in face and annoyance that you inter-
rupt   brought the tone down   I don't like being
a person. I prefer being a mind   All the tones
sound together wind-chime-like or raw-voice-graph
without having to understand   'I'm needy' 'So what?'

I pressed my forehead to my brother's bloody fore-
head in a dream and came away with his blood on mine
he has grey hair now when I dream of him he's

aged in death I've been helping him and vice versa
I remember dreaming the year before he
died he wore a short-sleeved red shirt
with a black stripe across his back and was
saying goodbye to his kids in my mother's backyard
Is there a beauty in as if the Oresteia my poem
Iphigenia is about us is the Oresteia more than grue-

some who did this to you or was it even done?
what was done who killed someone why is
another only "bent"   Do you know I was an advanced
archer?   The only important thing to say is,
And that when my father spoke to me at my door
it was as if he had to translate   So for the last oh
seven years   I've been trying to discover
how the dead communicate with each other
trying to overhear them   They and we holding it to-
gether talking everything talking mind

It Is the Ascension

It is the Ascension a national holiday
I saw an African lady in a long dress featuring Jesus
front and back within ovals she had Jesus on her ass!
She looked pleasant of face   I once had a dress that targeted
my belly with its pattern   when I was pregnant with Eddie
I hadn't noticed my doctor told me   but I only had three wearable
garments at that point this isn't what I would remember
I have been misremembering this morning a show two years ago
at the Archives Nationales   of manuscripts from Mosul
collected by Dominicans gospels korans letters calligraphy

in two alphabets and several languages I found it peaceful
I went back at least once métro Rambuteau cross a couple of streets
the writing floats in blocks of concentration and a willing
of this to be it the thought   the gospel the truth and your mentality
you are or would become the words their ornate spirit
say spirit as spir-it as Dolphy my old neighbor said Al-ice
to get real thought down and if you thought like a manu-
script I'm starting to organize my mental
experience into poems   hearing metrics for life
What I was really going to remember again, was when

in 2000, 2001 I dreamed briefly of a sunny island
I awoke and thought that was Tauris and wept
then wrote my poem "Iphigenia" with the Taurian version in
mind that she was not really sacrificed to Artemis so the Greeks could sail
to Troy but carried by the goddess to Tauris
becoming her priestess   At which point all human
sacrifice ceased though it hasn't and many are sacrificial
ones whom you know knew or are propagating the
form or enact it as I or mine   The new form on the island
simply to touch with a knife   the would-be victim's throat

and let one blood drop fall   I seem to remember the col-
lection of documents being in danger again as Mosul was
and the book that is not one's book and the careful heart

or mind of my text as I think it the art of thought
the Jesus on her ass would be part   I walked back from
the Archives past a shoe store and a pharmacy in July
there had been a staircase to mount and an older woman younger
man together and portrait boring of a patron as you rounded and entered
    the show
no one else there   oh a jacketed man carrying a motorcycle helmet
I was afraid then and am for Mosul and for our mind

Pigeon

I heard one of those pigeons or doves
it's hot for May but practically not in body I
sit vague and unremembering   I'm almost afraid
too torpid of the point of memory holding it all
so we can taunt each other with the past
the other planets hoary diseased forms

we were walking on . . . you cross bd Sébastopol at Châtelet
there was a loose crowd plus hundreds of demonstrators en-
gulfing street and sidewalk they were demonstrating
against demonstrations and strikes   I who was
weak and skinny from hep C suddenly cut through
them quickly leading my party across the street

and away in a long rust-colored summer dress
laughing   at the time there was perpetual strike
I'm so glad humans know how to know what
the thing to do is   Today no one's supposed to have talked
to a Russian just like in the '80s   I can't find you
you have too many dopey ideas and rules

gorillas sit endlessly eating leaves that's all
there is much boring footage   Someone was the greatest
writer this is known by its having been said
then you can believe or go on strike or eat
whatever's around   a gorilla remembers you
if you're nice and scratch your shoulders wearing twigs

on your head Dian Fossey Louis Leakey's women
you can get raped by an orangutan if you're
having your period   what I have to remember
is not to transgress where you're really outraged
at this point in time for no reason correct?
trying to find that condition that I actually am

how I hold you together by cohering as a one
I remember all the people who have been hostile to me
dogs on the leashes of themselves   who thought
it all up who are you   I remember we were lashed
into silence   and no animal could be god
I have broken through this crowd and I'm alone this time

I remember that room again the one of
everything   green and with no purpose
where I had never been born and my poems are
already written   if I can get to them from here
no one will let you through but I'm there
and I flow   and it's true that you have no hold on it

No Longer FBI

Agent Scully is going to shoot herself in the face
You will not be an agent for the blood-tainted red-
haired body secretly that runs the US and so the world
no I mean and I mean no more secrets . . . "you
don't know me" to the tune of "you don't own
me": Lesley Gore? Let's watch an episode of *The
Punsters*—isn't populist culture terrible like
the indifference of dreams? I will lead you from the
Planet of the Vapes or Rapes the hidden albatross-like
negative vibes, vibes apoplectic believers or
schemers, right where you, live   don't really live   live long I.
You are living live, get it? Can you remember that?

I realize I have changed and that the one I was to
become I am and even have been for some untame time.
There is hair on me a bitter growth that
comes not from the animal factory but my mind.
I'm reaching through your trauma to shake you up
Look at me I am your god if that be, the one who pours out
new particles from a no-face so you can re-
condition your existence and fucking grow up
I'm sick of your planet I'm sick of pretending
you can't do anything but what you do, pre-
tend. Pretentious, pend. A woman who can scarcely walk
perches on windowsill watching Scully with the gun
has her own bloody hair   is this about releasing *her*
from the service, the secret maybe ser-viss

is it would I be left singing particles
rush out of aperture in the language of . . .
so fast, not keeping . . . my secret's blown
that birdcalls resemble. Not keeping up . . .
Follow me anyway . . .

Change Sound and Syntax a Little Pronoun I

It's an old cigar box I found in the basement Diversey
St house that had been a nursing home
and where Ted saw a ghost   It has a black
clipper ship on it. I kept it forever
and put my stranger jewelry discards within
and one of the special pearls maybe. I took

everything out of it, about a year ago
and began to paste things in it just a
piece of white paper first   Then I needed
crystal beads I found a shop near
métro Réaumur   I only wanted a couple handfuls
they sold by a larger amount I'm

making something I said so she sold me
20 crystal beads. I wrote Box of Souls
on the paper then glued the beads down.
I glued in a rather large piece of quartz I'd
acquired in the '90s, and I found a clip-on
light whose cord was transparent—it

went in. Everything looks casually placed
and on the verge of changing position . . .
I don't know if it's done. When I close
it I forget   as I've forgotten to change how
this poem sounds from those before and I stack
things on it a Box of Souls. As all the souls in

the universe or anti-universe, having no size
being other than what we know could fit in there
the angels on the pinhead infinity in Emily Dickinson's
brain. Another recent one is a cardboard box encrusted
with paint and images queen of diamonds and green and gold
after positing a new universe composed of cubicles

and our choice of the fractured and rearranged pieces
of previous trauma experience and namings of parts
as if there were any parts   But we stand together
angelic at the edge of ice thaw over abyss to choose and remake
what we thought we once saw and did into our us the cosmos.
This is how I pass my time that no longer exists.

Rock

Place oneself out of time a body outside per-
ception   It's that room   But you're denying something
Fly over land which one
Whisper   you don't own me I am the holy
so I do the same things   because it's one time
getting on an airplane   so I can tell you

the language of and on the rocks   We put the
glyphs *on* but inside them who don't need breath
there is form a concentration of planetary hurt
volcanic trauma? I was always asking them—the rocks—
what they were. But I believed claptrap
of Observation . . . the difference between the living and not
et cetera. If we fly over that we can land and talk
it's blurrier than I thought   the photographs
of rock were only for my *human* eyes. I enter a cave
or structure of opening   and since it is inside me   for
I see it . . .   But you can sit down. We are not exact
it says. I know that. The reason you are failing to . . .
change *it* the present is that it doesn't exist. But
I will die of it! I reply   so I'm—No you won't, it
says. I know that too: I can't find the borders
of this poem   So I'm—I forget   You're, the rock or
cave says, greater than we are . . . not man but you.
What is greater? The pain now doesn't exist
for you; and you haven't hardened. Are you that
hard? I ask   It was so painful it says
That's how we know we don't exist   Who would have
done this, what would have—to us? And you
enclose us with your spirit   It must be made
less sad and terrifying I say   though you won't die
We are dead   Won't die. For I'm re-creating the
terms   on this planet   We are universal
I am universal I am re-creating
love, time, and all conditions   At the beginning, now
the rocks are unformed

Disclaimer to the Urgently Expressive

I disclaim all your experience as a small body victim
or member of a group   I throw it out
Talking to what someone found out among the particles
What year   I don't want to know how bad you feel.
The dusk-rocked grace bed is yours so shut it
Kicking out belief meaning and the apoplectic bullying device
I think that was everyone I was reading
they thought they were only connected to an only-each-other
though demanding every single person as audience
you have to say I'm hurt to every human entity to get rocks off.

I knew I was supposed to be supportive as if marching
But the best I could do was love everyone.
When the surface of the planet is dying though not the interior
You sometimes think the gnats should shut up.
They have souls too piling up in my souls bedroom
Alongside those of children dead of starvation in Somalia or Yemen
I was talking to you last night you had cast off your
Emaciation and babyness and had a clear light with eyes be-
Cause I know eyes and your parents had loved you
What did I do to deserve to be born among thoughts

That can be called thoughtless and purely mean
In the sense everyone is their thoughts?
No I wasn't born except for before birth.
It's hot today and I'm supposed to be in tune with my
Species—I'm sick of it, as it is, it must be changed
Into different thoughts   Soon you will have to
Give up your cars   no government but your own alarm
Will tell you to   Or flat desolation when there's no point
In "going there." I was born in terror and dis-
Trust of cars, and of people's assumptions

She told everyone to pay attention to *her* because
She represented *them*, or was it only because
She was she? The message is gibberish   the baby

Is composed of what I hadn't *seen* before as
Substance this it-is-just-love-without-human lang-
Uage. Back to The Old Language spoken by me be-
Fore I was born without what you'd call emotion.
'Are these just notes for a poem?' The language
My father translated into English when he
Spoke to me from death. Try to speak that, untranslated.

Doug—April 21, 2000

I was called by the nurse at l'hôpital Saint-Louis
'You must come immediately' 'What's happening' 'Just
come'   Later I made her confirm 'These are his last hours.'
I've recorded this several times in different ways   I
summon family from two other countries   but mostly I sit with
him—when I first sat down by his bed he
looked happy though was breathing difficultly
happy both to see me and to have arrived

at this goal. Later I'm utterly alone with him
and he who could neither sit up or walk for weeks
(I get back up, 2017, put on blue overshirt
writing can't keep up is too straight-lined)
he who could neither walk nor sit, sat up
cross-legged straight-backed, prostate cancer
metastasized into spine   and looked impishly like himself
It's you! I said (again, like with my dead father
when I heard him speak from death . . .)
He nodded, and proceeded to talk to the air in the room,
Called out a name or two—I thought he called
Ed!—Ed Dorn? Eddie?—but other words came out as
gibberish. Who are you talking to? I asked
and he shushed me finger to his lips. This continued
for some minutes, this confrontation with the
unseen; then he lay back down and relapsed into dying.

Later, others arrived and he lay silently. We
procured food from outside and ate—then I went to
take a quick shower in a bathroom nearby
Bonny came and got me while I was dressing
'He's dying,' she said. As I entered the
room the nurse was pronouncing him dead—I
seem to remember she was counting—can this be
correct?—and I shouted 'I love you!' He tried to
speak, I mean came back to life for an instant
and uttered sounds, then died. I hadn't even gotten across the room,

April of 2000, the first thing that quote happened
in this time period I'm reflecting . . . upon? or as
the poet says, being reflected upon.
The agency for thought requires does it inter-
action with the unseen   is think-
ing taught   does it start and stop   Do I think a dream?
One thing we did while he was so ill
was trance work together, lying in bed when
he wasn't in hospital—I was using trance to
write Benediction   And we would say what the vision
was together each contributing its details   a dwelling
at night with a lamp e.g.   Or there was a field of folk he said
And would *see* it, both of us, as real. As:
"these were people in a field. there was a rose petal on
each's forehead but it was later a ruby towards the
end of the vision. first we'd entered and stood in a cave . . ."
And I saw the parts he put in and he saw what I put—
we were treating his pain and trying to—be
together in experience which became as real as
a dream dreamed is, dream as real as life with-
out time. Where does thought come from in you?
Even if it ceases as something evinced be-
fore other living ones as of a nervous system
it cannot be *studied*, because of its subjec*tivity*
and there is no good description of a *thought*,
except perhaps in poetry. I would go back
to the hospital grounds and look up at the window
of the room where he had died. I wrote a lot of pages still, now,
unpublished; and forgot. Forgot as much as
possible   I didn't want to be so hurt again and it
was *his* pain   and kept it under where I've
thought without thinking and learned much.
I have no character I am a mind
I play at having a personality   investing nothing
in it   and Care for this body which we have all
dreamed up together—what we did with our *choice*.

The Answer Is Awe

Dream old pay phone ringing in hospital I pick up
receiver   voice says 'The answer is awe.'
Still don't know what to do with it last September right
before I was diagnosed   and the dream is still irritating
I have a checkup Friday   I'm working on The Old Language
again. Does do if it is there nothing or any thing
Take the laundry out of the machine—that proves zilch.
If the answer were awe, I would be burdened with awe

Infinity as a condition can't be some feeling
The Old Language is written all over and in me, but I'm not it—
it's possible I *do* it—She brought her friends home with her
this morning at 6 AM   hate her guts as we used to say
Jumble I it the machine   and question all   but the cancer
is so available   like so much isn't—good air and tranquility,
space between sets of particles   The particulars of this now
shouldn't be spelled as what you think you know

I close my eyes, and hands put a slender crown on my head
You cannot   I can't   restrain this passage of what
is not a self into further display   I should awe you.
Someone to convince that explanation must be dismantled
syntax unravels   and the bits that orbit around other
bits fall out of place.   While the newer languages
fell apart the old one golden as my fillet began to
spell Awe, and I don't know what it means. I've never

felt it, but perhaps you can. "I don't like this arrangement."
And then it's not named the area near the heart where
I was they said sick   But I knew that was caused by
my allowing your troubles and guilt to be inserted
within me, even as poet. This was The Old Language too
not as scapegoat but as song. No one knows why they the
tones work or even the microtones.
Trust them, the voice says. The Old Language re-

member   I was handed it in a library, a book but it isn't
literacy—that's only one version. Tell me the rest of
the stanza, proving that it's always within reach
anything could be it the people on the runway
spelling letters gesturally so the planes could land at night.
Somewhere else in the universe a rock speaks it
without affect. Or am I the one surviving speaker? But
the original must be in effect, always in place.

I Don't Like This Arrangement

Remember a year ago can you I'd come back from New York
and then the Seine flooded   it kept raining then stopped
I went down to look at it where the walkway was submerged
and not enough room under the bridge for a boat
someone's story about a péniche stranded   I waited
like a person for it to subside as if inside me

I wrote a poem about someone being a drunk, that didn't work
I found certain people intolerable   didn't want to
go out, I'd say   the mood from the previous Nov-
ember's terrorist attacks dragged on   'Let's go down to
the river' means my childhood and a poem I wrote for Steve Carey
(who cared for me)   it's not supposed to rise up and threaten

this is the new imbalance the crows speak of
in the park grossly arguing over garbage
I had dinner with a man who wouldn't listen
couldn't or wouldn't (those are two strange words
the letter combinations float away unreal as they are)
An explanation for anyone's shitty behavior   an ex-

planation exists for why our hierarchies cling on tell-
ing us whatever you think you want me to do
I couldn't write well because my interior city
the syntax would push me towards its maddened in-
evitabilities the poems' love was shrill   I dreamed
I got off a train at a station called Hell and was handed a brochure

by a woman whom I hugged at least she welcomed me
I've been here for the last year as usual it's okay but
nerve-racking   to become lighter more transparent
last night I realized that though nearly weightless
I had in fact healed the whole universe
and even this broken planet though there is a time-lapse

to consider you can't see it it's in another time you're in
like a future or slippage   But I had I'd done
it and still had to continue in this silly version
unwrapped day by day by automatons people
who can't know because they don't know how to
know anything except to obstruct each other

and scream for freedom as if it weren't there just there
even and truly   nothing left to lose   the one thing
who can't know and I racked and wrenched myself
so that you not really be here but there
out of your ridiculous imagination of a time and space
that you've wrecked   but you are the amnesiacs

Because

Because I don't want to stop talking to them the dead
It's always convenient for someone to dispose of them
I refuse to   I just start putting some words to-
gether c 2004 and I realize I'm realizing voices from
genocide who's telling who what to say why would
Anyone   want to be trapped in a body on earth
Hordes of warriors hordes of intellectuals as well, as self-

described   and sometimes there are beautiful
books do they have them on other planets
I remember Max of used bookstore 6th St maybe
with a tattoo from Auschwitz and blue marble eyes
Ted knew him he actually looked at me as if I
existed when I was *that young* but
none of those bookstores are there now

and the world is full of Holocaust deniers
another thing you can get away with as country or horde
I start writing *Songs and Stories of the Ghouls*
because I feel like a ghoul after the hep C treatment
Whenever I nearly lose my life I open out to all
the others in the wind   and since there are as many words
as souls or more I can work on their insect-wing-

encrusted gilt document I never intended to write this
or did always know don't you know   everything
about yourself anyone keeping the brakes on
Find a different version of Medea as culture-maker
lied about will return again in manuscript
after manuscript page she can even be funny
and Dido reclaim herself as founder of a city

don't you know the truth is plastic   No   Yes
being the illusion of your righteousness   Mine   No
Yes   and there is always a goddess sick of it   in
this case Maat the Egyptian soul-weigher turquoise wings

You the dead are not free for you beg me to speak for you
who of ones I never knew can find me there in
hermitage waiting for company dead I know

and don't know I will never pretend you don't exist
there is a you despite your culture all these beliefs we
think us and manners of being the best among made-up standards
and of compensation   What's that for   whatever was done
when nothing ever needed doing
Oh us   Fuck us   I have come to you to keep you warm
Her auction name was Grace and she is my friend

Safe

I wrote *Culture of One* almost consciously as an adieu
Go back   I was upset and serene at same time
Starts with that dream, sure   Of the cloud out-
Side the old drugstore dark and with armlike ex-
Tensions I'm afraid of it that a dark man walks towards
The drugstore from whose bookrack I bought *On the Road*
Was the cloud the cloud of unknowing?
It's Mercy, I begin, sick of her job her self-knowing as Mercy
Jack too—I saw the Beats show at the Pompidou
Last summer and engaged with 66 again and artifacts

Of my pressed-dust times old colors gas-station orange
But I'm talking 2008 right now   Homage to Marie
The Self-Sufficient to Marie to me to the desert
Of knowing   clear light sharp faceted blue and brownish
Unknowing in heat-driven solitary necessities
40 days and nights in the wilderness child's play
I invented Marie's story   but she didn't have one   you
Don't have to   I did the only research I could   asked
Old ladies what they remembered   No grave marker after her
Death by exposure to heat   The most interesting

Fact courtesy of Bernice via my mother was that
Marie was happy   in the sense Bernice said that
'She felt she was doing her thing'
I'm looking at the book now it's so beautiful
I wish I were writing it maybe I am and it's still
Then   'It means that I make perfect sense'
Me Marie Momma and Bernice   know what we're
Doing Eve Love is starting to Leroy does
And the Satanic Girl   but does Mercy? she's
The most trapped   Does the desert wren with its crystalline cry

Do the dogs I'm not sure   ever ruined by humans   I and
To go down by the water to baptize myself myself
We are locked in a language of nerve endings neurons

Mercy thinks pain is real though and responds to suffering
In The Old Language everything is both sacred and fluid
In mine anyway and pain is more dreamlike trans-
Itory   I've never been tortured except mentally but
Or heartbreak the clichés come back festered
Jewels whose colors drip off   'Whose little girl
Are you?' the witch asked her daughter in *The Burning Court*

Bernice in her house smelling of garbage sur-
Rounded by cactus Marie bag-ladied at dump   Momma in
The house I grew up in but I I began seeing an
Imaginary house as mine with silver-framed photos
Ancestral portraits the house burnt down later in my imag-
Ination I have no house now I'm Mercy   with-
Out a statue even   I became her not myself
Philip Whalen might get it   I'm the cloud the arms
The object of my initial fear M or A
"Victims of horrors" your world will not succeed

But you are "safe in heaven dead" without a mirror or despair

From Dream Notebook

Dr says I'll have to flee will tell me when. a dream
one of those clinic dressing/undressing rooms—
try to figure out why   what flee what go where I'm
all there is will be can't get rid of   "Dr says I'll have to
flee will tell me when" is what I wrote down
But Friday I seem to have written "I just don't under-
stand what you're thinking of / you're sad, you're thinking of sand"
The night before *that* I receive clothes for Night Woman

who's that whose dreams are these whose life in which
if there's really such a thing as a year   Write
better Okay you are dilapidated formerly No
I had been running where petunias grow sticky
bewilderment of mastery as symbolized by my
Cappadocian soul house dream on the alley about a year ago
But in so-called 2005   in so-called 2005 I was writing
Negativity's Kiss of which the heroine Ines Geronimo

was me too wasn't she   I didn't do any research
I let the words flow out of my fingers one of
the characters was modeled on Bob Dylan a has-been
one was Rupert Murdoch if he were in Batman
one was all the nutcases I've ever known and cum
French philosopher one a vain MFA poet one a bi-
racial cop one a sweet secret agent as if one of Eckhart's
agents that is—intelligence? Hurricane Katrina intruded in the middle

and now I remember the Brainard–Padgett booklet en-
titled *100,000 Fleeing Hilda* (tasteless)   and don't want to run from
anything Ines wouldn't   but who am I not to
run from the cities that give me cancer for example to
where   Am I exemplar of the outbreak of a disease the
doctor actually said the mammogram was good on Friday
in this poem of actuality picking and choosing the words
of pre-catastrophic strophes   higher waves

of chaos and the Night Woman forcing you to sing of sand
the Night Woman expands the new constellation or black palace
I can't find a daily expressiveness after
2005 Ines was my last public woman as heroic
accompaniment to people's working out of their cul-
tural and political fates   I mean everyone
nation and tribe and whose infinity in what grain of sand
whose beach to waltz on in our pathetic costumes

Survive

Possibly my life has been too easy since I've survived
I was never sure I wouldn't end up on the street
I mostly didn't think about it I had to write this
I probably thought the street would be okay though later
realized the gods or whatever had a plan for me
I could still fuck it up not by selling out I'm too old
but by killing my neighbors maybe it's possible
no one would even notice never noticing much

I'm trying to remember when I started to like it here
maybe after about my 15th year in this building
maybe "liking things" isn't what I do or do
it later in the remembering process I'm enacting
I remember before so many machines it was hard to
be as noisy   Doug telling some baby American tourists
to shut up at 3 AM from our window down to the sidewalk
'You're naked!' the girl said 'What difference does that make?'

1993   I remember realizing c 2005 we'd still had to
entertain ourselves from ourselves when I was growing up
though I'd sit by the console radio   But people sang
gave recitations, made chalk drawings to piano
accompaniment at church   I learned how to play
the upright piano my nephew now possesses in Tempe
Perhaps because there are billions more people they are call-
ing attention each noisily as if earless by now hoping

the vibrations are enough I've gone into mind spin
The plan evidently has been for poetry why so I
could at a certain point explain my talent who
can't get your attention adequately though I'm cor-
onated—the machine will kill me that isn't a word
You are suffering you don't have to I'd say if
you listened you chose it you chose your form
you chose your evolution and certainly the bad

weather you most especially chose to be cruel to each other—I
wonder if I should again try to break my neighbor's window with a rock
Why was I born you say   Were you I say
You've been listening to what has already been said
Call yourself a baby   call yourself a child an ado an adult
who has to have a job   No call yourself this location or
vibrant mass in a paradise of connection ever ex-
isting to be because there's no not-being   It is all

really other no body 'They're so noisy' some no-name
wind will blow their noise away   ('They take me up in their
dimpled hands and blow my hair away')

Creating the Memory Collage

Because I was mourning Doug so hard   but push out onto page
Alma, or The Dead Women   I couldn't then react too
to 9/11   and I have placed it where I'm not but visit it's
flat pressed into the ground through plexi-
glass a diorama die pun the medium herself can't
handle   my sons there Eddie later worked as security
guard at Ground Zero   I tour the smell of the relics
with Anselm   I had been unable to locate

locate them at first   from Paris but I was calm   two months later
dreamed they were harmed   you put it one place it comes
out another I was outraged I was supposed to dot dot dot
Why bother with the topic   I can't do everything can
I   Trust the words now it's all I have
Years after sent the emails received from my sons and their
friends   as a historical document   pages from Karen
long poem from Mariana   fear and love more of love

and from others too I meant sent to my archive at UCSD
as history   In *Alma* away from the ensuing wars
we re-make ourselves in a Needles gully the years
of the burrowing owls   Alma whom I am and owl
shooting up heroin into her forehead is god the
primary with pantheon   ah Mira Myra Anna et cetera
Anna had been real in the sense of actual person a
hooker in Chicago run by John the Pimp oh that's

another story but in "Anna Shoots the Biograph"
(theater where John Dillinger was shot) she and I
were killing our biography   I assumed her
dead of AIDS by then only saw her once she might
have made it   a beautiful African American in a red
coat and makeup   repaying me for valium lent
to John for her coke crash Anna I've always remembered you
where was I all I want to keep of it love and words

and the incredible thoughtful resilience the depth of
goodness—la bonté, caritas—in my sons
on the zen wind the ever-ness of a skill to say

Presenting Thought   The Old Language   Ocular Migraine Comes

"To move is to write to die is too"
"I am a world leader"   I said writing
if every action writes, amazed to be here
(Ted, I think)   You keep rehearsing therefore,
I'll get around to it, presently, I'm
in 2011 I believe I go to Cork first it's cold

what remember pizza parlor coffee shop
stay with 4 men Oh right festival at church
churchyard grass which readings miss why is
he so noisy   these words are it and not it thought
is thought even a thing   is a thing a thing   you keep re-
hearsing at the end of the second act and cold buy

a white shawl   of bamboo fiber   In Cork?
By the time I go to Needles   (one hundred twenty-six
degrees there today)   to say or write it, which one is
it more   reading Len Deighton's Faith   Hope   Charity
the 3rd spy trilogy about the fall of the Wall
there is no barrier between is it me and the dead by this

time I like this arrangement   but I'm about to do
castle battlements Right Now is this writing stress-
ful *at this minute* making colored geometries in eyes
'there must be something I don't want to remember'
I dreamed I felt bad when I was there or 'd just returned
it was a feeling bad in a dream in that house I'd grown up in

I dream I'm dreaming then wake up go in living room—
oh go away colored lights of an ocular migraine—
Daddy's there it's morning and I realize I have no cause
no personal cause to feel bad it's the universe itself that feels bad
That's why it's trying to distract me now with colored
lights   from writing   don't you get sick of

psychic phenomena can't tell them from any-
thing else   she gave me the ring that summer

the one we'd given to her   for her 80th birthday with
all our birthstones my real birthstone is—
the lights are stopping—just some rock
because I'm a world leader   do you have a legend

as the spies the written ones would say   I was at
that time writing about being as poet a spy
then the Wall falls and I'm not a spy anymore
Larger than the universe   which is only sensual I
am   Take me or leave me   about to be sick no
feeling pretty good after all and the greatest of these

in The Old Language you don't have to explain

And then again looking for a recent past that is a present thick
with time past and to come so you know what you're
doing in a fact . . . the idea of a spell or hex . . .

that you can be bewitched   came into my existence, again
in Paris as the extensive mind I am
Europe's recent witches are rural and often men
it's more like you curse them your neighbors
I read a book . . . read some more books
it's the saying of the word by a sorcerer
the word of trouble and death   and you find out it's you
and become sick breathe badly consult a dehexer

who viz advises you to wear a St. Benedict medal
          when you go out
or fries salt in a skillet   forget what for   But all of
human activity is it nothing but sorcery   I believe I
have enemies surely in poetry   do you
yes though they wouldn't own up   how can I
put this people don't want you (me) to be as I am
but more primitively practice magic naming us any-
way   I'm protecting myself with amulets sure

and writing them for you   as any poem might be that
those who are after me . . .   But would never admit
as a village sorcière never says   and in the mind that is
the poetry world there is witchcraft practiced per-
vasively   naming of the so-called facts of the so-
called villains denunciations and makings of lists
who's good or bad do you get it the word as death
are you white or black   is one's use of a word so power-

ful that you must avoid that word on yourself at any
cost   I can't avoid words any words and wear a St.
Benedict medal   whenever I remember
because I am blessing you   and have the power being
alone   people in groups hex each other   and persecute
the outsider too but *one* outsider isn't really part of the fun

Was I partly living alone so I wouldn't hurt you
Too hard to explain just protecting myself from ap-

proved malice   There are nothing but witches everywhere
all social groups cohere in sorcery   Political parties surely
but arts movements zeitgeists and fads at universities . . .
you know the verb   Or that one word comes after another
so sometimes one's work is in fashion
"There are several women who unconsciously want me dead"
I know who they are who you are in this theme worked
out in my life since I was ten

Trying to Get to Desert Hole

I find out I have hepatitis C and two hours later
give a poetry reading at a Paris bookstore
I get piece of paper test results—is it raining on paper
then put on pale blue top to go read from *Alma, or The Dead Women*
I'm fragilized as the French would say
other or half- memories press in sketch lines like when straight
lines are graphed becoming arc of a circle—
but you don't have to believe it, geometry   thin was I sick

I couldn't drink wine without feeling it too much
especially in the desert walking behind local ball-
park searching for burrowing owls everywhere
2002   read *Desert Holes* also trying to get to you
inside the owl's physiological head another owl
bunches of thoughts/lines/phrases   more show up that aren't
the curve   I'm inside the owl's very head
inside the feathers/skull/tissue where the eyes look

at me and I am them too   Very inside must I leave
and enter the description of sick of malady   The owls
holed up around the rim of the gully   once a nest on
the high school lawn   an owl flaps her wings to
divert me from it   Aunt Margaret, always
on the animals' side says leave her alone
But I'm trying to get to you   Do you remember
now says my doctor in French   how you might have

caught hepatitis C?   I injected amphetamines in 1970 and then
forgot   I did it for about a year but it wasn't very im-
portant to me not as much as owls these short ones
rather long-legged living anywhere   *Desert Holes*
says berms what is a berm and the light and what
is cultivated for no reason   I'm reading
from manuscript always at the Red Wheelbarrow bookstore be-
fore it moved to métro Saint-Paul across from a hidden passageway

the voice is always stronger than I am coming from
somewhere other than the physical equipment as out-
lined in text   living floats around the body
but something of me as well directly inside you
or I in the bird's head   no such curve a de-
scription   Hôpital Tenon at métro Gambetta
the lover of a woman who had worn long black gloves
the lines or phrases pile up   but the curve will never

be exact as I remember it   in the Hustler's Dream
could you be lowlife in 1970   it wasn't really
in my repertoire   what was? how will you ever
live? I'm amazed to be here   there are windows in
the owl's head vents or lights a safe space she's not just
flight she may be trying to get to me after all
having no question   in The Old Language I am your friend
footnote: ornamental olive, hollyhocks, petunias, periwinkles, etc

Doug's Prescience of His Death Louise Michel on the Bus

In 2005 editing Doug's *Whisper "Louise"*   I'm looking at
today June 28, 2017   to find the dream on the bus . . .
2005 *Whisper "Louise"* ("Every little breeze . . ."
Maurice Chevalier) only flash memory walking rue Bleue
leaving la poste with proofs in summer   I'm calling on
the dream though   1998 and he was writing *Louise* but

we were vacationing in the south I was writing *Reason and Other Women*
had located an 11th-century monastery Mont Canigou   for *my*
book's purposes   in the eastern Pyrénées   you went straight up a
    mountain
and inside, members of a religious order   both sexes   prayed
in nontraditional garb I remember as being of white and purple
But the night before, Doug had dreamed of Louise Michel and
    Théophile Ferré

figures of the commune   sitting across from him on a New York
bus Ferré speaking Louise staring   dream Doug took as premonition of his
own death (he was diagnosed with metastasized prostate cancer one year
    later)—
Louise looked at him that way   And after we left the monastery
Doug who was driving our rental car (I can't drive)
became almost crazy on the steep cliffside roads hairpin turns

fearful that the premonition had been of a car crash that day
and he might take me along   poets are lunatic like that
you might say   I calmed him down and we spent that night at—
can't remember—so high up where he continued to obsess somewhat
After his death in 2000 I left Louise's photograph on the wall
for several years   she wasn't a bad tutelary spirit and I

had visited many of her Paris haunts with Doug
have repressed though or turn from details of the memories
just, we went there: the ballroom at Ménilmontant, her grave,
a certain library, a play about her, a prison in our quartier, where

she was held   all of which segues in my mind to Doug's hospitals later
and the utter foreignness the French tongue surrounding his

death these hôpitaux with courtyards   Catholic chapels
At métro stops with names from another history than
my own   He died at l'hôpital Saint-Louis near métro Jacques
Bonsergent   but had had back surgeries at l'hôpital de la Pitié-Salpêtrière
métro Saint-Marcel   A hospital named Pity
And all the while, Louise! I typed the last chapters

when he could no longer sit at his desk   I think the
prison was the one formerly behind rue de Chabrol
in Passage de la Ferme-Saint-Lazare   and I suppressed
having seen it, you see? until I discovered it for
myself in order to write *Our Voice: A Bible*
The town in the Pyrénées Mont Louis I now remember France's
          highest fortified town

The question   is there one   would be of violent revolution
or change   Louise was grand and complex of
extraordinary stamina   not so Ferré   but dead
is everyone equal   and we visited near Neuilly where the
German army first encroached in 1871 . . . or at her grave across
from Asnières in the same cemetery Maurice Ravel

I can never be "French"   and is Frenchness a thing
can I be without qualities opinions—violence or
I *am* revolution involving no genocide   I'm of
no culture now but was I once having come from the Mojave
who *has* one of those—a culture   I bought Doug
a gant or washing glove, as requested by a nurse

at La Pitié, on the boulevard Auguste-Blanqui yes another communard
La Pitié was where, as I wrote in *Culture of One*, I
sat by his bed and read aloud from my manuscript of *Benediction*
It's beautiful a woman said in French knowing no
English   sitting by the bedside of her seriously injured son
in the same room   did she even know what I was reading was a poem?

Crown and Cancer

The crown is complex layered matter   in image
quasi turban because thick and round but goes *around* not over
'to help you grow into it'   mental equipment but I'm
retreating from my animality acquiring more brains
Then literally to become everything   Dogs howl across
the black sky purple heads of and I don't leave

The subsequent dream's banal a poet
lets me out from her car alongside a wall
barely enough room   Later I vomit   Getting rid
The crown makes me sick   so much mentality
for a body   And why did I also have to get cancer
To put more pressure on   actually to help me sur-

vive until   and it was small   so I can enlarge
Does anyone else understand what I'm talking about
I'm at your bidding but can only tell you
These weirdly calligraphed near non-existences
In the corner of my heart is a coin to turn on
The tumor near my openness my aperture

where at night it seemed the dead inserted their
surviving unhappinesses into me   *That's* why there's
a nearby breast tumor   *Fantasy*   The world
is *your* fantasy I say to you   so ugly of
compulsions   *must* do this or that con-
nected by grimy strings the conception of the plot

I never confess don't you see   there was nothing there
You are a reliquary   of ashy old thoughts encrusted
with flowers rock crystals the treasure of the abbey
2015 at the Louvre the black knight is Saint Maurice
the silver one with jeweled cap Saint Candide
Everything I have is mental   and my manuscripts

too many are *your* real reality   the collection of precious
parchments the holdings of the library
nourishing the souls of the un-literate
you just don't know how to think how to tell
how to *happen*   I exist to relate to you the largesse
you would be if you left the scummy words you use

and followed beyond money back to home
the bodies are all coincident one covered by pearl and
gold and ruby and sapphire and emerald mind
Or collaged the ripped-off previous images of attraction
You left you scatter you look back you fight
each one a diamond light inside are you ready to go

Nobody got it   Lying there postoperative the truth-key 2016
too drowsy to eat or go back to my apartment I did both
I'd dreamed I probably had it, before the diagnosis
You have to have one more shot   (like a hep C shot)   a voice had said
In another the nurse said we're going to give her very tall flowers
It's just that it was near where nightly

They deposit their dreariness and I remake it
into new soul   release as gold-and-green secretly
the new particles the new microtones into the uni-
verse re-creating it because I can   It's too old and sad
All of it   You found the material irresistible like
a bet you lost and I I'm picking up the pieces who else

Dinner at the Prime Minister's

2005 receive dinner invitation to Matignon think it's a hoax
RSVP my friends advise I do so   a club I've just joined, for
international poets will dine with the prime minister and his wife
so I go   fabulous Versailles-like rooms   introduced to Dominique
de Villepin premier ministre also poet we eat at tables for five
I'm trying to recall my table an African a Belgian an Indian
Mme de Villepin sits with us to begin with then "works the

tables"   we are trying to figure out when to start eating she
says "attaquez" dig in   Later a friend of hers a classical Spanish
singer plays the smallest guitar I've ever seen and sings wonderfully
A writer from Cuba reads a poem someone I know I for-
get who reads one or two more   de Villepin makes a speech
about the importance of internationalism and poetry

it's good the speech   it isn't dumb or superficial
he means we all talk to each other across borders and
poets know how   Around 11 p.m. we shake his
hand and leave   No one knew who I was except for
a couple of Frenchmen   Was I the only American
I think so   I wore one of my dark pantsuits

no one had known how to dress and I
discussed this with the Belgians   who were men
almost everyone was a man except for Zoe from Cuba
But now I remember talking to a French editor
a woman at my table   The African poet—a man—
had a wonderful name like Apollo or Zeus

though he was ordinary looking, nice   Was the Indian
poet a woman? I don't think so I just remember an Indian and
talking to that person there were many Africans there
Michel Deguy was there and got cold (I think it was March)
maybe he read I was otherwise living in my state
of loneliness still the current one   on the other hand amazed

quietly   about a hundred people   I think I ate fish
how could this have happened it was delightful
it helps to have a palace a big food budget   and there were
no consequences   except that I can tell you
about it here and say I am an international poet
our locality is now the whole planet   *I am*

an international poet in touch with the poetry worlds
of several countries—do they have 'countries' on other planets?
I value the parochialism of my room on rue des Messageries
as I loved Needles and St. Marks Place NYC but
the fading or bleeding into each other as we hack at
others and so-called Nature breaks my heart

"you saw it coming" over and over
or did everyone see it coming   one could con-
tinue blaming countries or whoever (you
were *all* a bunch of sexists no one gets off)
Your phones for example sheer escapism
Take your faces out of your phones

Look around for christ's sake   Look at what's going on

Carte de Séjour

2012, '13 I have been in Paris for 20 years
I hate to admit that my French isn't wonderful I'm
unassimilated but definitely some sort of immigrant
in this syntax where one is definitive subject and verb
I think I'm avoiding   There's a new bureau for re-
newing one's papers at rue du Delta near rue Pétrelle
almost at Barbés very near me   Last time 2002
I'd had to go to boulevard de Sébastopol at 6 AM stand in line
for 5 hours outside the préfecture with masses of
people Asian African Middle-Eastern the world is every-

where mixed up now   I shared a blanket for warmth
with a woman from La Réunion 10 years older than me in '02
but in '12 I only had to make an appointment
and buy a 200-euro fiscal stamp   Then Anselm Karen and girls came
and it snowed it never snows   What did we buy
in that funny pharmacy hand cream and vitamins   Anselm and I
walk in snow at night discussing the US State Department
Sylvie and Anselm on ferris wheel at Concorde in snow
I watch with Karen and June who has a meltdown
in the Louvre the second time after seeing another long hall of

paintings coming up Anselm's Caravaggios
this is to say, that they inhabit me
wherever   the girls break my pink mechanical cockroach
and wear out the battery of the owl whose eyes flash
I live in Paris I just do am I supposed to
live somewhere in particular the ghosts
call me back here not historical or cultural
but essential what calls on me what can find me
Here   they those it living in these quarters
where Sylvie and June might also jump on my bed

I will only ever have these rooms. The world is owned
Paris is called owned and pressing on you would buy you up
An older immigrant hopes for a future still

is that it—you have too many questions in your
poems, someone said   I prefer the interrogative the sound of it
I went to a store and then I went to another store, is
that better? or, I loved, I despised, I resisted . . .
you must have been fortunate to have the strength
But their disjunction was unlike their stable positions
Is matter stable? or, matter is stable

and over and over can matter exist without memory
our memory my memory or its then, if all
there is is memory   how is it shared and called gravity
in 2002 the sari'd woman from La Réunion and the Middle Eastern man
he who remembered me from the first time   that is we'd
unsuccessfully stood there having come too late
the three of us now stood abreast I bought us news-
papers at one point so many in line the woman from the
préfecture came out and shouted hysterically Don't Push!
'We're being treated worse than dogs' one near me mutters

pushed together pushed together like molecules

Breast

One of the occasions you're the actor of yourself
and good in role   or rather like when you're born and you're
supposed to cry so you do thinking 'I don't want to
cry for them' I almost remember that
A peculiar I mean they were watching my right breast
I was sent for a biopsy but no something small
has shown up in a whirlwind in the left they biopsy
that   Do you like this the word choice and it's cancer
when the surgeon tells me I make sure I can schedule the surgery so
I can give all my readings in the States then I cry
just a little in a dry and luminous way a short desert storm
but I don't come to care about it *that* much last

fall was it   I had tried to figure out how I'd react be-
cause I *knew*   but mostly being an annoyance I'd
have to go through it was given short shrift—I like
that expression   I was fairly certain I wouldn't do chemo
the ones inside me I consult with said so
they said I had too much to do   But I remember
after the diagnosis consultation blood being taken   my sputter-
ing out things in French while a technician not finding a vein
repeatedly   gave me over to her more adept supervisor
If I were a mainstream poet here I'd come up with a metaphor
for my skin being stabbed and hacked   if experimental
I'd not write this poem   if a prose writer I wouldn't be im-

patient or rich in point-of-view complex observation
but all I mean is everything   *you* can't do it (don't
do it, don't do it)   But, I wasn't going to be category
and no, I don't respect yours   I don't respect any
religion choice of garment set of manners or emotions
I was lying in bed last night realizing
I am composed of power lines in thick bundles
red-gold trajectories not nerves or in pathways
not same length or anything consistent
I'm courting this what I am as well as a thought system

not localized to me nor dogmatic like human
has become   Or was that what thought was always for

to impose upon oneself and others a way a way and style
The dominant human mental state may be smugness . . .
So I had the surgery went to Tucson San Francisco
Philadelphia   and New York where I lost my wallet in a
fit of uncertainty   or *for* one   I *had* to mime a condition
came back to Paris and proceeded over weeks to radiation therapy
tattooed strapped in and zapped   Can you hear it the poetry
Up that hill each day place Monge small rues then rue Érasme
(My mother had read *In Praise of Folly*, which referred to
farts her favorite thing)   then rue d'Ulm l'Institut Curie—
they invented radiation!   it's icy January
A small club of women waiting   the technicians are just kids

I like the big guy because he handles me well and the young
woman who is friendly and changes hair color weekly
You know this stuff   You know   everything like this
I don't know how we got here   in meticulous relation, to cancer for
     example
and I detest reacting   those the two things I wanted to say . . .
machines and drugs heal you   but when I had thanked my
liver doctor for healing me of hep C—that was years ago—he said
'You healed yourself'—and I've known all along
I was healing you, reader, though I was a patient
it's what I do every day now   I've nothing else
left on the quotidian vanity level   or
to call myself something as someone   'she was . . . you know . . .'

Uncle

Because I was too much too far into remembering
I forgot what else I had been doing
Starting to read the hideous New York Times International
then hanging laundry I was remembering Woody
and how Spanish was used by my family for swearing and difficult goodbyes
'Estoy aquí para decir Adiós' he said to me in 1999 not knowing

who I was   No I want to recall what I did in 2013
After   and then it was   do you need to know after the January of
snow the breakdown of the hot-water heater and my plumber
possibly beginning dementia   inherited from mother he was afraid
But I am writing the first volume of The Speak Angel Series
I go to Prague and to . . . Cedar Rapids, Boise, Missoula, New York

this can't be of interest   bought a faux leather jacket
washable I still haven't   each in his or her difficulty   out there
I told a messed-up version to Ed Skoog of the rich animals with a butler joke
punch line: 'Mr. Rab-*bit* is taking a shit'   But I can't ever go home
that is to Needles where Mr. Tur-tle (down by the well) the desert tortoise
dwelt in the backyard   the year Momma broke her hip

2008? a snake took over the tortoise's hole and Momma was scared
to come home from the rehab till it was gone but . . .
And Woody was anecdotes by then, whenever
He is Carmen in *Alma, or The Dead Women*
for his full name, my uncle's, was Carmen Woodrow Williams
and I refer to him in 2013 in The Speak Angel Series Book I

there isn't one time or year for this aggregational
thought (cf Bob Creeley's intro to Whitman—the
dirt spheres 'aggregates' Arthur Okamura showed him on the beach
at Bolinas)   In 2013 did I have enough money
With my tiny pensions reversions from Doug's death
and now social security (2015) I can probably make it if I stay here:

claustrophobic apartment and French health care
estoy aquí . . .   Woody was nearly illiterate you see
and begs the question of the written poem   suddenly
I don't know what a word is   and letters lose their reality
he had been a cowboy, a construction worker, manager
of a Flagstaff laundromat   he wore a cowboy hat

and generally had a horse, could be difficult Aunt Mary
cut up his boots once in anger (scissors? a knife?)
but he swore in two languages continuously everyone loved him
and I was thinking of him a few minutes ago
couldn't remember where I was Paris   The other kind of
memory a past reconstruction   and not of where you are

I don't know how to remember how to be here
in Paris   ('Keep walking   Keep walking'—*The Descent of Alette*)
I must go outside again to figure it out
No one will know who I am   do you exist
only in the gaze of others? in the mirror? philos-
ophy crap   I am beautiful existence roadrunner, scorpion

I am the swooping-down owl of what will come

Imaginary vs Dreamed

If an imaginary house burns down that had been your imaginary
house for years   and without warning it burns and you see
the fire in your imagination you're left with a pile of burnt
boards   they seem to be on the coast of Normandie
though resemble the black boards left for years after
the Cry House burnt down in Needles the Mohave Cry House
which had been where you turn off to go to the Marina
(Natalie Diaz will know) it burned down right before we moved there
in 1949   'What are you talking about?'   My
house of self burned down   so did the Mohave funereal dwelling, once

and someone will try to get me to spell Mohave with a 'j'—
Listen, it isn't a written language, nor does it resemble Spanish
and they called themselves 'aha Makhavi'   But back to coastal fire
Since in my imagination I was left without walls
by the Atlantic 2014   my visionary house has not been re-
placed because   I am not like others   I've always
treated my real apartments as temporary   I've lived
in this one for 22 years I know I'm home in the world
within mine or my sons' apartments when I see Schneemans
Brainards Burckhardts on the wall we share a floating

international apartment in air
When I was a small child I dreamed repeatedly
that our house was slowly on fire and I couldn't con-
vince my parents or siblings to leave   I would go in
and out but couldn't leave without them
Now there's nothing left and that's all right
just of my own but as for the world itself in slow flames . . .
And the Cry House would have burned fast
I put it in a short story I wrote when I was 21
from the point of view of a man not Mohave who went there

to mourn a friend but went there finally to cry
the small flames in the world poke up in the ice melt and ocean
I have a source of energy for everyone for I

am perfecting a description of mentality—what
there is—and how I use it to remake us   A smooth
grey-black stove of a wood-burning type burning nothing
now stands in dreams but not my imagination
in a Cappadocian-monk-type dwelling
on the alley, it must now be the alley house cf *Mysteries*
of Small Houses I have become clean and obvious

But in my imagination that's not in dreams I'm homeless
I might have an ancient fortress on a hill but
I don't seem to climb up there   I sit on the beach in a sort of alcove
facing the sea white sand—Do you want your own house?—
And no one needs anything—Do you hear me?—
You fools you don't need to be helped! You're al-
ready dead   Pressing me the newly dead ask Is
this it?   Yes, and it's fine   smooth birds balanced
in no air   over the shoulders of what we've
taught ourselves images and structures that

I'm remaking. out of the ashes? where? in my mind
in this same apartment, 21 rue des Messageries, Paris, France

A Month Ago

As everybody knows Mosul fell   I am full of your
souls   the only afterlife is inside my mind
and I neglected to caress you mentally and love
you last night though my extent is always open
and you crept in   People make and destroy things
They demolish enemy cities old buildings and ar-

guments relationships and cars   As everybody
knows an entire ancient city has been toppled
frightened-eyed women with their children run
or a man carrying a baby photographed for
my benefit and a prize   Like the books and manu-
scripts the precious objects saved several years ago

rescued conveyed away could the people not have
been placed somewhere else before the all-
important demolition occurred that signifies ISIS isn't in charge
how did there get to be such a thing as position of power
concept item the rent paid vindication   Righteous ev-
eryone is   don't tell me about your politics ever again

who oh anyone alive   The dead say We are sorry
about you for you have accepted us there isn't room
Yes there is but the human part of me can't inter-
act with each one of you yet all are welcome for I am
your space   Your beliefs didn't prepare you for me
but I think you begin to understand   Yes they say

it is the enlightenment without our details
But we were always here weren't we   It could be
the closet I hid from the warriors in   But it, you
is are so expansive   that I can relax into all of it he says
I have accepted the dead killers as well I say
Everyone or -thing was always the same in its lack

of conception its wisdom in infinity its grace
beneath and beyond rules and teaching I'm just here
you have come back to me   This is power
a listening and without tension or organization
as you have known it the star can be
behind a cloud or not   the point where you

replace yourself with yourself

As

As when I wrote the poem "Your Dailiness" about 5 pages long
I woke up one morning age 27 and it was there I
knew what it was and spent the day writing it down when-
ever I got a break from taking care of my child
I forgot for a long time that this had happened
I knew every word of the poem already though the
entirety of it as typed didn't quite resemble what
I thought it looked like almost but not quite . . .

I think most of my poems may be already written . . .
partly written? or the space for that poem is there
in time as conceived as more spherical than linear
so that you sort of already know what will come
About 2016 last year, I started to be aware of a vast green "room"
with no walls floor or edges   pale green in which
there was a stele or slab large   dark or bronze
that the poems were already written on but with an

ongoing change of individual letters like an old-
fashioned railroad time of departures board you
know with the clacking change of destinations and hours
It's there, changing just a bit at a time till you write it
down   Some part of me always in that room with the
stele a word which I had never had to say before
it sounds like the marble but I'm stuck with it
that's fate what are you going to do with this information?

It's possible the poems are written in what I call The Old Language—
I dreamed in 2016 I was in the stacks of a library   probably the
Needles High School library a man handed me a big old
book with The Old Language stamped on the cover
I guess I think that there's an original language
that everyone and everything is, throughout the universe
that I translate *from* when I write my poems
I can't seem to see the language on the stele though

I don't seem to know The Original Language, or
I do and I don't   It may be too opaque to be a lang-
uage as we understand that word   It may be
a force's particulars   wouldn't need an al-
phabet but one would be possible wouldn't it
I live in that room too I'm standing there I've
always been there   But I have to be here to write the poems
I have to go through all this—why?

Is It Fibrant or Vibrant Death

(George Romero has died)   A voice says 'I really don't
want to be the one who knows'
I say 'I have to be the one who knows'
then must find out and control
the smallest bits   the atoms of the spiritual
a piece of a letter of the alphabet said or

how are you thinking what really   Eddie and I watching
famous oud players randomly hear that *that's like it*
On YouTube   and quartertones I have an Algerian song
on iPad (album: Fighting Songs of Algerian Rebels) called
          Remember Of Dead
What does *that* mean I can't seem to internalize microtones
that I believe I *am* more and write *in* like here

Go back. It was between that and that
When I was 5 or 6 Momma taught me the Hopi Corn Maidens' Song
which over years I changed   put in European modulations
Near her death she sang it again sounded more like
Remember Of Dead between monotonal and quartertonal
cf. Tina Turner has sung the same Buddhist mantra her whole life

Eddie picks up his guitar and plays oud-like 2017
If we're always doing it are our so-called bodies?
Science thinks symmetry but I don't   'Are these just notes
for a poem?' Maria said . . .   Are we just notes for
a universe?   But I only really think when I write
Eddie also thinks with a song perhaps   Tina per-

ceives love when she chants she says   she's brilliant
There's a light to emit from person people talk of
the metaphor I hate that word   Night of the Living
Dead triggered something like a breakdown in me
in 1972 my atoms seemed to disattach from each
other   couldn't move   the model wasn't working

I say 'I have to be the one who knows'   keeping your
shit together   or not   because if you fall apart as too I
nearly did in the 1970 Jimi Hendrix anecdote, on acid . . .
it isn't all right but can't happen what is it
I've almost got it down 2017   'you always knew'
So I could be the one who knew   because I had to

Sight

That I would have trouble seeing
That it would be peculiar to see   that you
can only *see* me   you can only *sense*
me what word is me
we're no we're inside telepathy or *nothing*
would work   don't you see

we have to be inside each in order to function, so
remember that time with Marcia
when we smoked hash and in each other's minds
reacted to Tony Serra's part of the conversation as one person
driving to Berkeley that was '68 I put it in my poem,
Eurynome's Sandals 2006   it was an experience I didn't like

the border between our two selves disappeared—
you're supposed to like that I mean then
you were supposed to   as in the LSD bad-trip
experience when as I said later I was hanging on to
myself by a thread   and my smug peers said
you should have let go of it . . .   I *saw* the thread, silver

I like my character Eurynome   the goddess who danced
the world into existence in the Pelasgian creation myth
Not about seeing you say   My vision started to degrade when I
was six there was the blurry world and the *glassesed* world
was there the immaterial world   thought as sense . . .
hating the woman downstairs and her noise

Help   we have not further to say   caring as a sense
crying as, through the tear   you comprehend
a more heightened sight clear and is it mus-
cular—I had to do eye exercises once   Do you read me?
detached retina '79   when all your senses
collapse   do they leave an impression on your *soul*

an ability or disposition towards   or did you have that
before you entered this world
as the presumed body with your given name?
Eurynome in my story is not very clear-cut physically
brownish, blurry   a deity   she visits other planets
has an affair with a snaky film-maker who's two-timing her with

The Jealous Woman the star of his film of the Apocalypse as it occurs
other characters a shaman, a monkey, and The People
They're not just doing it with their Senses   not The
People but any group being a group   They ar-
range themselves via an ordering
of a part of Chaos or Void, say   that is, The Old Language

they clamp down on it and make it *theirs*   then
you born of them have to be *theirs*
you have to see hear smell touch taste they told you to
would you if you, what? I just sit here
I just walk down the street   fold it up fold yourself up
like the dead tyrant is folded up at the end of my book *The Descent of Alette*

Then remember how to be from before you were born
I wear contact lenses and they are that   I dream some-
times that they're enlarged or jagged
Now I remember I *saw* a page of
The Old Language two nights ago   right margin ragged
I would *be* that   only be it   There's some other form

My Favorite Phrase I Don't Care

I didn't care who wrote anything   or what they thought
it was boring   as boring as politics   I mean poets,
not clear clear I don't care because it's not there
where you think it I'm going to enter it now and show
you and how nothing's dangerous   it's a door   this time be-
neath the surface of the earth and with a green X on it

the souls are kneeling I can't my old knees hurt
oh you're kneeling to me   it must be a joke   No
we're trying to show you something in The Old Language
we are *of* you and need the care of your heart art whatever
we are the ground itself   but how I say can I believe this gro-
tesque thing   It isn't belief we've been here waiting

for this moment for it seems forever though we do other things
So what happens I say   We *are* they say The Old Language
what you speak now   it not what it means though that
might show   you've been learning it from us in dreams for years
I can't seem to dream right now . . .   Because you're now ful-
ly conscious   I'm sad though   And one kneeling says

Behind your body you aren't   You're now the expanse of
the that which you show without knowing: Now know
But why   And they bend lower awed face to ground
Face the ground you are   You see because you're ex-
plaining to us   in this enactment and the black
robe fits you and the crown to say beneath   so   say:

I broke myself for you now I'm too old   yet I'm
the whirlwind bringing the destruction and chaos you
seek   for you can't answer or accept the charge
yet all the information is where you are
you exist exactly where you are alive or dead a
fine mess   your face is atop   that can't survive

Dreaming While Awake

I have had the dreaming while awake ex-
perience since 1998   it's boring to explain or
so fucking what   but I will be in my 'waking
life' and dreams will beg to intrude not hallucinations
but dreams, that is, contained *other* experience from one's
interior not exterior projections or visions   a dis-
tinction no one gets when I try to describe or again it's
'why don't you like it?'   I don't like it   my con-

centration in both worlds compromised I rarely
remember the dreams but I can't do my wak-
ing task correctly talk to you or give a poetry reading
The experience often comes with jet lag   But
there's a whole other world of voices and images calling
Once on an airplane Paris–San Francisco   I sat
with my eyes open experiencing a dream of a man
in outer space explaining a screen with a globe on it

the world? you're not supposed to cross so many
time zones? I've given at least two poetry readings
in the States while I was thus dreaming I don't
know how I managed with the interfering image buzz
it's like falling asleep between words, get it? Trance-
like rhythms can trigger the experience reading *The Descent
of Alette*   or reading from Beowulf in a workshop
Do you like this confession? can you understand it,

stupid? No?   Ergo though, I'm being beckoned to by a
parallel world I'd forgotten I looked up Angers this morning
as destination for possible trip   that was where, once too
I'd gone to read, via train and in the gare Montparnasse
the dreams clicked in   cavelike greenish shops
I was that time really in caverns of knobby colors as
I dreamed awake   Trying to learn from it   Where are we
Why did we decide on this one, this world

I encompass too much do I for this body
Dreams as a way of thinking . . .   The Old Language
the visual puns   Are you a visual pun my dear
I mean deer with a diamond no rhinestone collar
I have been calling forever back to the voices
calling to me trying to say what it is
interrupting my tranquility I can't have that
I think I first saw in the gare Montparnasse the cubicles

I'm proposing as the building blocks of the new universe
How far back can something immaterial extend
how green dark green light green   We need
an entirely new composition in our universe we're
now inventing under my aegis are we and on
that parallel plane the new reality   there are two of
each of you and one is there   whirlwind coming I'll have
to like it more—or will we even notice the transition?

Anselm Hollo

What year one time we went up to
oh you know those brilliant wildflowers high
in the Rockies red and blue overwhelmingly
Anselm could drive a lot better than when he first
learned in 1972 'I like to think of a car as an
extension of myself' as he crashes a no-parking-

zone sign in front of our house in Chicago parks then carries the
sign inside (what is a sign   the dead told me yesterday:
words don't mean the same things for them the dead don't
want to refer to the same kinds of things)
Anselm Hollo and I are driving somewhere in the Rockies
we are high on talk we can do practically an-y sub-

ject except sports which I could do a little—I
have a standard entrée into e.g. boxing
Anselm only likes to read and talk books and gossip
he is probably translating something a biography
of Strindberg or German detective novel the Turk
in Frankfurt my son Anselm, Eddie, and David have read

all those   Try to be more particular   I have Femara fog
so is that poet that everyone thinks is so nice is he I don't
think so I say I don't think he's such a nice guy
And the story of the one who punched the other out
while driving don't try that Anselm (I seem
to remember that once when drunk he offered to punch out—

who was it and then   the time Armand Schwerner
thought Anselm was laughing too much   during Ar-
mand's reading of *The Tablets*—which *is* funny)   We really don't
have to go anywhere   We go to used bookstore may-
be the time Adam DeGraff is with us   and I buy a beat-
up Ross Macdonald   It was very hard when you died

I tried to help you get there though I was 7,000 miles away
leaving online messages a hospice communication ser-
vice you and I each saying 'All there is is communication'
There are these people Eddie said that it's always the
same with no matter how long it's been   since you've
seen them the same space of knowing them forever he meant Anselm

I want to refer to that reality changeless there were
no gaps   we never owed each other a thing
somehow we had separately been through everything
without it becoming our history   but the memories
have parti-colored flowers in them and un-
changing light   everything speaks without time passing

it's just that you were always interested in what I had to say

Jimi Hendrix Anecdote

It happened in 1970 but I didn't know how to
tell it until 2005   Now I don't want to tell it again
but it belongs I'd like to tell it without telling it
(as in heaven)   It is as I've said in the other po-
em that doesn't quite tell it a benefit at the Village Van-
guard to Free Timothy Leary   Bill Berkson and I have
taken acid together—Sunshine—I've taken a half tab and come
to this room with a stage in its center   I wanted Ted to

be here he isn't but Anne Waldman is Wynn Chamberlain Sally
Henry Pritchett and the people who speak and perform Jerry Rubin
and Barbara, Alan Watts—carried up on a litter
he is ill or crippled—and Jimi Hendrix   I enter a bad-trip zone in
head and feel I'm at a real crisis I might 'lose my mind'
in the sense *you* who? can 'lose' it   Henry's face melts
and I can't speak at all   everything onstage is a drama it's
psychic stage central in shadows Jerry Rubin makes a

desperate-sounding speech—Vietnam?—he and Barbara
in tableau like actors shouting at end of world 'Oh
Barbara' Anne says from audience   Hendrix later
comes up plugs in guitar performs solo, no one plays
with him or is his entourage   Finally at moment I
stand mid-room people starting to leave and I'm
frozen concentrated on keeping hold in head of
small white thread that is myself   I'm holding on

and Hendrix walks up to me then past but first looks
directly into me seeing what I'm doing   I just
stare, still focused hard on holding on
Bill finally takes me out of that hell-room
outside instantly I'm no longer high   a few months later
Hendrix is dead   There is in fact no anecdote
no one saw anything except Hendrix he and I
were both there in it a mental point of communi-

cation it happened   and on my 60th birthday I
tell the story to Peggy Tom Marion Joe Anselm and
Edmund   But do you see how fragile and strong my
what was imaged as thread was   and how Hendrix was in
passing the only one who saw where I was at
can it be that easy to lose   and if I hadn't held on
what would become I would be annihilated
was annihilation a real possibility what would it be

this thing that happened this is this thing that happened

These Are the Clothes of Night Woman

You will always have light limbs even old
and you can as if fly   these are their materials
she said handing them to me   but was a younger woman
and didn't care   When my mother was dying and
couldn't really walk   and ate like a bird or insect
I tried to feed her canned salmon cakes bits of pasta

the house a nest   for sixty years   no I'm What
Woman walking behind a dark Mountain on streets
I'm Frightening-Mountain-at-Night Woman
my garment is a thin weave of granite
And before I was born alive   aged all ages in
The Big Green room I foresee this time of re-Creation

My arms are around all you   All you and I
as if flying extend myself past night into
neither day nor night   these are the clothes of
that one   They fed on bits of manna and   wore
or were gossamer   like moths   they *were* their clothes
I've forgotten to have any dreams again

I am enlarging as all that silliness dries up
and falls off my surface oh what you do to me
you have conspiracies against me in the official myths
but I'm so far beyond outrageous fortune
that I remember not even being born
I'm going home my mother said

but first she spoke of Pentecost
when everyone was understood in their
language   and my garment is of those words   The
Old Language   that alloweth me to move and fly
to still run in the park as if flowing   to expand though
holding you not dreaming interknit or woven

and I found my parents I'd already known
to be born in the myth of the Alley or Everywhere
the life would be sacred almost an emblem and bleeding
so the colors wouldn't stay   I saw that the
materials of the universe   were unstable not factual
and were inside the or my soul   the purpose

of the senses would be growth *through* them
you can see that we a chaos cohere
no matter what we *do* if we redefine matter
And I will see you and see you again holding
in the borderless way   and becoming *in*volved in mind
No I'm in the green room with the clicking board

announcing the words of my poems that can change
upon the instant like at the train station
this word came up Inexact   or the famous
Changing Woman   foreseen and I'm omniscient
I mean it's *my* time in here   I'm in control of
The Old Language   what I am   it's always *my* time

About the Author

Alice Notley was born in Bisbee, Arizona, on November 8, 1945, and grew up mostly in Needles, California. She was educated in the Needles public schools, at Barnard College, and at the Writers' Workshop, University of Iowa. During the late sixties and early seventies, she lived a peripatetic, outlawish poet's life (San Francisco, Bolinas, London, Wivenhoe, Chicago) before settling on New York's Lower East Side. For sixteen years there, she was an important force in the eclectic second generation of the so-called New York School of poetry. In 1992 she moved to Paris and has lived there ever since, though retaining her ties to the United States, to New York, and to the desert. Notley has never tried to be anything but a poet, and all her ancillary activities have been directed to that end. She is the author of more than forty books of poetry. Her book-length epic poem *The Descent of Alette* was published by Penguin in 1996, followed by *Mysteries of Small Houses* (1998), which was one of three finalists for the Pulitzer Prize and also the winner of the Los Angeles Times Book Prize for Poetry. More recent publications include *Grave of Light: New and Selected Poems, 1970–2005* (2006), for which she won the Academy of American Poets' Lenore Marshall Poetry Prize; *In the Pines* (2007), which inspired an album of music by the indie duo AroarA; *Culture of One* (2011), a verse novel set in a small desert town; the "everything book" *Benediction* (2015); *Eurynome's Sandals* (2019), named for the goddess who danced the cosmos into existence; and *For the Ride* (2020). Notley has also received the Griffin Poetry Prize, the Shelley Memorial Award from the Poetry Society of America, an Academy Award in Literature from the American Academy of Arts and Letters, and the Poetry Foundation's Ruth Lilly Poetry Prize, which recognizes the outstanding lifetime achievement of a living US poet.